To Mom & Dad,
All my
love,
Julie
(April 1983)

The Rockies

Andy Russell

Hurtig Publishers
Edmonton

Hurtig Publishers
10560 105 Street
Edmonton, Alberta

ISBN 0-88830-094-8

Printed and bound in Canada

The author and publishers gratefully acknowledge the support
of Alberta Culture in the preparation of *The Rockies*.

Captions for preceding pages:

Crowsnest Mountain in Crowsnest Pass, southwest Alberta, so named
by the Blackfoot. Legend has it that a Blackfoot war party surprised a
smaller number of Crows here and gave chase. In the ensuing fight the
Crows were trapped between the mountain and their foes and were
threatened with annihilation, but they took to the cliffs and disappeared.
The Blackfoot held the mountain in awe – a condition of mind that was
reinforced by the Crows' escape.

The exquisite detail and rich colours of the forest floor form a natural
mosaic. The browns of needles and cones shed by a variety of conifers
towering overhead are livened by the bright contrast of tree lichen.

The golden mantled ground squirrel is generally found at high altitudes,
sometimes above timberline at 8000 feet or more. Not as gregarious or
numerous as the Columbian ground squirrel, more than two of this
species are rarely seen together.

Lake Oesa in Jasper National Park lies cradled at the foot of rugged
mountains amidst moraines, talus fans and lingering snowdrifts.

Soft light filters down through the thick, interwoven green boughs of
Engleman's spruce. Unlike the rain forest farther west, the forest floor
here is relatively uncluttered.

The late Buck Dixon, famous trapper and guide of the Yukon Territory, was standing with me overlooking a vast expanse of mountains in what is now Kluane National Park. It was the early spring of 1959, one of those breathless, sparkling mornings without a cloud in the sky, and the peaks, fifty miles away, stood out in sharp detail with no hint of haze. We had paused in the midst of dall sheep lambing grounds and the slopes around us were alive with them.

Buck was a rough-cut character with an even mixture of Indian and Irish blood in his veins. Ordinarily he was not a philosophizer, but something about the scene must have reached into his soul that morning. He replied thoughtfully to a remark that I made by saying, "Man doesn't own the mountains – they belong to the bear and the sheep and the rest – man is only part of it."

Buck's life had revolved around trapping and hunting for over half a century. Some would have accused him of being a heartless exploiter; others might call him a waster and renegade. Maybe he knew he was dying, though it was more than a year before he succumbed, a victim of terminal cancer. I remember him as one of the most skilful trackers I ever met. He was also a very entertaining and amusing companion, but it was his power of observation and his flair for interpreting the small details of the country that impressed me most.

Like him, I grew up amid mountains – the Alberta Rockies – and made my living as a trapper and guide. The passing years left their imprint and I came to know the fruitlessness and frustration of seeing but not wholly understanding my surroundings. To walk or ride across the mountains merely to reach a destination, ignoring the features of the country through which I passed, became unthinkable. But the more I observed the more it became obvious that no man could ever read all the inscriptions of nature and time on the face of this rugged land; one might only interpret a part of it and the attempt to do so becomes both challenge and fascination. One cannot walk half a mile in the mountains without encountering a host of signs, evidence of things living and long dead. In them lies the utterly enthralling story of nature – everything from the contour of a solid rock formation to the fragrance of the most delicate mountain flower.

To become a true naturalist takes time, time spent in the wilds recording and organizing various observations until there emerges a pattern of life that harmonizes perfectly with the land that supports it. It is an exercise in interpretation that may be mastered only after years of experience and even then the task is never complete. My own forays into the field would not have been possible had not my wife and family shared my interest and often pitched in generously to help. Nor would my work have been possible without the help and cooperation of a great many friends and associates.

Today the nature observer's power of expression and his ability to record detail are enhanced by the magic of photography – the medium of applying light to the emulsion of highly accurate colour film through magnificent lenses of the finest technical quality and past a shutter that will freeze the beat of a wild duck's wing. The timeworn adage that a good picture is worth ten thousand words still holds, but in this book we have combined the two mediums to capture the meaning of the Rockies to this nature observer.

The text cannot begin to describe every detail of the illustrations, but in many ways the pictures speak for themselves. Their locations encompass a wide area of the mountain country, for the Canadian Rockies stretch from the forty-ninth parallel to the Arctic coast and from the eastern foothills to the Selkirk Range. However, the theme follows in large part the main range of the continental divide, the spine of the continent, where at some knife-edged spots on the ridge one can empty a pail of water and send half of its contents down the east slope to Hudson Bay and the other half to the Pacific Ocean.

It is a country rich in history, both natural and human. While the arrival of man is comparatively recent, his presence has wrought tremendous changes – changes which have in places altered the features of great mountains. It is a country of enduring, magnificent beauty and a splendour that can tax a photographer's skill to the point of desperation. Light changes are so swift at times that despite speed and attention to mechanics one encounters frustrating defeat. But there will be wonderful golden days as well when a cameraman can seemingly do no wrong and the results are a joy to behold.

Photographers are something of an unusual breed, particularly those who wander the wild, high mountain country of the West, suffering storms and countless other hardships which nature sees fit to drop on them. They are a physically tough and persistent people, possessing almost limitless reserves of patience and endurance. For all their resiliency, however, these photographers are no less than artists, basically gentle of nature and truly in love with their subject material. That love shines in their renditions of what they see, imparting a spiritual aura to their photographs that elevates photography above the faithful recording of detail.

And because I am one of them, though not nearly so skilled as some, this book reflects my lasting respect and appreciation for their work.

Each day in the mountains has its moment of magic. It may come in the evening when the setting sun caresses the tops of the peaks with warm rays of light and colour as though bidding them good night. It might be the opening of the petals of a mountain flower, welcoming the sensuous probings of a furry bumblebee. It may be the sight of a thunderhead's towering column, its mass like carved ivory against the deep blue of the sky as it builds itself on thermals to a height of miles. It leaves its lasting impression as one stands beside a murmuring river under a canopy of a million stars, the infinite depths of the universe framing the peaks on every side. These are the moments of witchery experienced by those who live with senses tuned, seeing, hearing, smelling and feeling the ever changing expressions of the mountains. One understands then that time alone limits the knowledge to be gained and the discoveries to be made of nature's mysteries.

For to be sure it takes time to develop appreciation, understanding and love. Unfortunately most of us are in too much of a hurry trailing something called security to realize the benefits and gratifications nature bestows on those who side with her. We spread ourselves thin and travel the world's pathways at a frantic pace, yet often we fail to catch up with the happiness so avidly pursued. We encumber ourselves with possessions to the point of paralysis. We create ugly scars by tearing what we want from the good earth. We do not see that the earth would gladly give us much more if only we cared enough to be gentle and to take more time.

To contemplate one of the great peaks of the Rockies and perceive only a massive, shapeless rock is to be blind to the fascinating history that is written in its strata. A billion years ago the continent of North America was being born. It was a slow and stormy process with the land's general outline taking form in a great ocean's watery womb. The climate fluctuated from one extreme to another with occasional floods inundating exposed silt flats. Roaring rivers flowed down from the heights of land, tearing loose vast quantities of pulverized rock and building deltas. There was no hint of the Rockies then, only the rough-edged Pre-Cambrian Shield and a few ridges and isolated mountains standing adamant in the face of the floods. Each of the watery upheavals deposited a layer of silt of varying depths; the ripple marks and mud cracks of some old beaches are still perfectly preserved in the sedimentary rock, hardened by the pressure of its own weight.

Slowly but surely the land began winning the war with the water, lifting and assuming a distinct outline. By observing the signs left in the vast layers of rock laid down as sediments and volcanic lava, we can piece together the story written by nature over the ages. But in spite of our accumulated research we are not completely informed. Old concepts are set aside by new discoveries. Geologists are not in complete agreement on the age of the Rocky Mountains; furthermore, it is possible that the formation of the Rockies was much more rapid than first believed. But regardless of the length of time taken for them to rise up in jagged outline against the sky, the reason for their appearance is plain enough.

They are the result of a crumpling of the rocky plate covering North America, a movement known in geological parlance as continental drift. Its westward thrust produced an effect comparable to that of pushing an uncooked piecrust across a smooth tabletop until it encounters some immovable object. At the point of impact it wrinkles, bulges and folds back on itself to take a vastly different shape. Somewhere to the west there was apparently a barrier holding back the general drift, a barrier that consequently caused the earth's crust to heave, fold and fault itself into sharp-cut ridges and peaks. And lo, we have the Rocky Mountains.

The forces at work were gigantic and cataclysmic. Great ridges were pushed up, sections of some collapsed, and sometimes the formations even overturned. The valley of the north fork of the Flathead River in southeast British Columbia shows evidence of such overturned stratas in its outcrops. Mighty overthrusts were created when the earth's crust heaved, broke and slid for miles over the surface. One of these stands paramount – the Great Lewis Overthrust, with Old Chief Mountain projecting above the prairie at its tip, near the international boundary on the east side of Waterton-Glacier International Peace Park. The limestone formation of this mountain has moved an estimated twenty-two miles from its original bed.

In many places the whole crust is thus lapped, such that if a drill were to be passed through the formations of a mountain peak from top to bottom, it might end at precisely the same formation in which it started. What a motion picture could be made with the use of animation and actual scenic cinematography to illustrate the birth of the Rockies! It would be of tremendous educational value and would spark an awareness of geography among people like nothing else. Many craggy mountain faces expose in cross section millions of years of earth history.

Between two billion, three hundred million and one billion, nine hundred million years ago, the only animal life was aquatic – the simplest and most primitive one-celled variety. But it was abundant life and the fossilized remains of millions of these tiny creatures make up the bulk of the great Rocky Mountain limestone formations found today north of Crowsnest Pass. South of the pass in the Waterton area pure limestone formations are rare, for here most of the sedimentary rock is colourful argillite, a slate that sports every hue in the rainbow.

Gradually some living things left the water for the land. Life was becoming more diversified and complex, and every creature left signs of its passing. Between the Jurassic Period, one hundred and seventy million years ago, and the Cretaceous Period, about sixty-three million years past, exotic jungles flourished amid steamy swamps in a tropical climate that was incredibly productive. Vegetation was so heavy and lush that vast quantities of it accumulated in the bogs – the beginnings of our present-day coal deposits. It was the age of the great reptiles, when the dinosaurs, brontosaurus and other exotic creatures, large and small, abounded in the marshes and jungles. In the only major gap in the Rockies between the forty-ninth parallel and the Arctic slope, where the Peace River meanders through a corridor about a hundred miles wide, dinosaur tracks have been found perfectly preserved in the solid rock that was once a mud flat on the edge of a swamp. (Before any real study could be made of their significance, the whole valley was flooded by a power dam constructed across the river. Few people cared then, but some day when the dam lies obsolete, the Peace may flow free again and the story of the dinosaurs revealed.)

By the Tertiary Period, roughly one million years ago, the land had won its battle with the water. The continent had assumed its present shape and fertile grasslands predominated. Unable to adjust quickly enough to the climatic changes, the big reptiles had disappeared and their numbers replaced by herds of warm-blooded mammals. These ranged in size from five-toed horses and small camels not much larger than jack-rabbits to massive creatures – great hairy mammoths with enormous tusks and, among many others, the brontotherium, an animal constructed along the lines of a rhinoceros with a blunt, forked horn on its nose. There were sloth bears, saber toothed tigers and giant bison in this colossal circus of strange and mighty animals. Some went the way of the dinosaurs, others migrated west across the Alaska-Siberia land bridge to populate Asia and Europe. The fleet little horses disappeared, but their larger descendants eventually returned by boat with the Spanish explorers.

Meanwhile, the Rockies reared their heads, new, craggy and sharp-edged – a vast, tumbled mountain chain flanked by minor ranges all the way across what is now British Columbia to the Pacific coast. The climate continued to cool, heralding the coming of the ice ages.

There were four distinct glacial invasions which flowed down from the north and northwest. Now the mountains stood with only the white crests of their peaks showing above a vast sea of glittering ice. The ice plowed its way southward slowly and relentlessly, smoothing the contours of the country as it went. The mountain gorges were carved into U formations, loosing the sharply defined V shapes of water-eroded rock.

During the first three major glacial periods, there was one ice-free corridor left open. It reached from Alaska, passed through the Yukon, and then bent south through Alberta. Despite this corridor's sub-arctic climate it remained a thoroughfare for men and other animals now drifting eastward from Asia across the same land bridge and south toward warmer country. The fourth great surge of ice barred the door for a time, covering the corridor with ice a mile deep.

When about ten thousand years ago the great cold spell ended, the climate turned milder and the glaciers finally retreated, the work of the ice was revealed. The meltwater lifted the levels of the oceans, flooding the land bridge that joined the continents between Siberia and Alaska and leaving only the tops of the mountains exposed – the Aleutian Island chain. The features of the Rocky Mountains were less harsh and the valleys between them much wider. Today fragmented jewels of ice still hang in the high basins and larger glaciers still choke the heads of some of the valleys. The rivers wind down from these in braided channels and the plow marks of the ice still show as scars on the slopes above the valleys.

I have stood in the timberline basin at the head of the north fork of

Kintla Creek in the extreme southeast corner of British Columbia and marvelled. For here the country seems to have only recently emerged from the ice, as indeed it has, for the creek still wanders across flat pans of exposed rock unconfined by the channels and canyons that it will cut for itself as time proceeds. In the middle of the valley, amid groves of feathery green alpine larches, stands the Nunnatok, a rock edifice nine hundred feet in height, carved and shaped by the abrasive action of an old glacier.

A few hundred yards up the creek lies an exposed limestone reef. It is composed almost entirely of hundreds upon hundreds of tons of fossil collenia, an ancient vegetable of the algae group that grew in the intertidal pools when multicelled life first emerged. It was cabbage-like in its layered structure but its leaves were pointed like a giant asparagus tip. A modern variety still grows in the tide pools of the Great Barrier Reef off the coast of Australia.

This valley is a continuing delight – not only a pristine and remote wilderness, but a track reader's garden of Eden. One can view the signs left by living things that flourished in the very beginning, the marks of more recent ice and the fresh hoof and paw prints of animals that evolved after the time of the giant bison, sloth bear and mammoth.

I found a fossil collenia that had been split lengthwise by frost lying in lush green alpine growth, its cabbage-like layers exposed in detail. Within sight, a few yards away in the damp sand by the creek, a big grizzly track showed so fresh that particles of sand along its sharply defined edges were falling into the depression. It was a rare opportunity to observe the evidence of two living things thriving in the same area but separated by millions of years – a link written in stone and sand, illustrating the vastness and insignificance of time. Who are we, that we should be in such a rush?

As though possessed by devils, we pursue those trappings of material wealth we think important. We worry, rip and tear in our frantic accumulation of things. Yet as I stood there pondering the fossil and the bear's paw print I wondered if nature would not contrive, over the millenniums, to soften and hide the scars we have created, to heal these wounds when man, as unable to cope with change as the mammoth and the sloth bear, would disappear. But unlike them, would man be the victim of changes wrought by his own waste?

My companions and I shouldered our heavy packs and headed up towards the top of the pass. As we neared its summit the unfolding vista of mountains beyond revealed the massive Kinnerly and Kintla peaks to the south, both over 10,000 feet above sea level. Trapped in a hanging basin between them lies Kintla Glacier, just a mile or two as the raven flies beyond the international boundary in Glacier National Park, Montana. But our path did not lie in that direction.

Turning, we climbed west up the steep flank of Goat Ridge. The footing was bad here, with the loose, weathered rock sliding and rolling under our boots at every step. But as we approached the knife-edge of the ridge top, a goat trail materialized out of nowhere as goat trails are inclined to do in such country. It offered us better footing along the way we wanted to go – towards a secret pass artfully hidden on the spine of the ridge.

Years before I had discovered the pass from the far side by following the other end of this same trail. It led across the coarse scree of Ptarmigan Basin, disappearing as if by magic at the foot of a thousand foot vertical cliff that seemed absolutely impassable to anything on two legs or four. Yet when I reached the cliff a ledge made its appearance by sheer sorcery, illuminated by the light striking the pitch of the mountain face at precisely the proper angle. The ledge sloped diagonally up the cliff so gently and easily that with a bit of patience and effort one could push a wheelbarrow up to the top of the ridge. There the goat trail takes a step up about three feet and goes through a narrow slice in the solid rock barely wide enough to accommodate a man.

As we reached the ridge this day from the opposite direction, the sun broke through the clouds to light up a vast panorama of peaks in every direction. Behind us lay the tumbled reaches traversed in the last two days backed by the wild, high mountains of northern Glacier Park. To our left the steep-pitched flank of little King Edward Glacier clung to the north face of Sawtooth Peak, the only remaining piece of old ice left in this stretch of Rockies south of Mount Assiniboine. To our right and below us, bisected by the ledge, was the Painted Cliff.

Its name is self-explanatory, for it is a mass of brilliant colour – contrived by the growth of rock lichen – a multitude of hues ranging from black to brilliant fire orange through red, blue, brown and all shades between. They are not soft pastels for the most part, but gaudy pigments splashed lavishly on the rock face in a design that defies description. It is indeed a rock painting acres in extent. Let those who think man invented what we call modern art take a look at it, and they will quickly realize that nature has been an impressionist painter for thousands of years.

Lichen is a plant that multiplies itself by spores only millionths of an inch in diameter. It evolved through a kind of marriage between fungus and algae – fungus that supplies the acid which breaks down solid rock into soil, and algae to provide the organic matter that the fungus needs to survive. One of the most primitive plants to be found in the mountains, lichen is the first to appear on barren ground. Very slow growing, it has been estimated to take a hundred years to spread itself over a square inch of rock surface.

As we paused there considering how best to photograph it, we wondered when it had first taken root in this place. Again we were confronted by the inconsequence of time as measured by the life span of man. When the ice retreated, leaving the Rockies freshly scoured and sterile, this was a spot where nature's gentle caress first brushed the face of the mountains to restore life among the peaks.

1 In the winter of 1898 J. N. Collie and W. Wolley made the first ascent of this lofty peak, Mount Athabasca. From its summit they made the initial discovery of the vast Columbia Icefield.

2 A panorama of mountain peaks along the continental divide marking the Alberta-British Columbia border. This aerial view shows clearly the sloping strata created by the thrust of the earth's crust at the time of the Rockies' formation.

3 Soft sedimentary rock carved in delightful shapes by the action of the Vermilion River in Kootenay National Park.

4 Peyto Glacier, part of the Wapta Icefield, shows the graceful flow lines of its slow progress. It spills its drainage into Peyto Lake, and both glacier and lake are named after Bill Peyto, one of the first guides of Banff National Park.

5 Bennington Glacier in Mount Robson Provincial Park – one of the most picturesque in all the Rockies. In summer its spill waters form a sinuous channel, not unlike a twisted silver snake, in the valley below.

6 A hot weather stream of meltwater flows swiftly over glacier ice.

7 The toe of Robson Glacier above Berg Lake, illustrating the bold outlines carved by its own action and the harsh influence of the elements.

8 Looking down the steep slopes of Victoria Glacier above Lake Louise from Abbot Pass. This glacier has claimed the lives of several climbers over the years including that of Phillip S. Abbot, killed in 1894, after whom the pass is named.

9 Mount Louis from Mount Edith overlooking a valley vista in the Rockies of Banff National Park.

10 A thunderhead hovers high over the Watchtower in Jasper National Park.

11 A climber rappels down the awesome face of Mount Edith Cavell.

12 The west slope of Cascade Mountain in winter with banners of snow flying in the wind off its summit.

13 The view of Mount Robson's north face as seen from Robson Pass and showing the broken line of the serac across the top of the glacier.

14 Mount Assiniboine, the highest peak in the Banff National Park area, displays flags of mist flying from its craggy flanks. This mountain bears a remarkable resemblance to Switzerland's Matterhorn.

15 The high cliffs of Castle Mountain in Banff National Park stand like gigantic battlements among sifting puffs of mist. On a prominent rock shelf, half-way up, there is a small overnight climber's shelter often used by mountaineers.

16 A coyote in its heavy winter fur lies resting in ground drift. One of nature's most adaptive and intelligent animals, the coyote has survived man's attempts to wipe it out with lethal poisons, traps, hounds and rifles, and is still found in good numbers over a wide range of the continent.

17 The black bear, another animal that has learned to cope with man's intrusions.

18 Sleek and healthy, a mature cow moose lifts her head to munch a mouthful of aquatic vegetation picked up from the lake bottom.

19 The animal with springs in its legs: a graceful mule deer doe cocks her sensitive ears as if trying to locate the sound of the shutter.

20 The mountain traveller often hears the piercing whistle of the hoary marmot among the broken boulders at timberline. The marmot shares the hibernation championship with the ground squirrel, sleeping nine months of the year.

21 The beaver beckoned the early explorers who were mainly interested in plundering its pelt. The fur trade almost exterminated this big rodent, an animal that can tip the scales at eighty pounds or more, but sensible management intervened to save it.

22 Few scenes speak so eloquently of the northern Rockies as a caribou bull etched in sharp detail on the skyline.

23 Once found from coast to coast and from Mexico to the Alberta parklands, the elk is the second largest of the deer. A most enterprising animal, it competes with all the ungulates for range, except the mountain goat.

24 A Canada lynx, seen here feeding on the carcass of a mule deer, may have taken over a wolf or cougar kill. They habitually prey on rabbits, grouse and mice, but when necessary will tackle and kill deer and wild sheep.

25 Canada geese resting during their northward migration in spring. Ofttimes in spring and fall, the mountain traveller hears the deep-throated honking of migrating geese.

26 A svelte, well-dressed Bohemian waxwing. Males and females of this species bear identical markings and colouring.

27 The common loon is a handsome bird and the largest of the divers. It often nests on mountain lakes at lower levels, generally laying a single egg.

28 A spruce grouse photographed at close range – not a difficult shot to accomplish for they are quite tame.

29 Few animals are more entrancing than newborn bighorn lambs. Playful and remarkably active from birth, they are often seen running and gambolling on steep terrain where a slip could be fatal.

30 The black swallow-tail butterfly, most often found in country above 4000 feet in elevation.

1

3

4

5

6

8

9

11

10

12

13

14

16

17

18

19

20

21

22

24

25

26

27

28

30

Sunshine and Storm

From the very beginning, the greatest single influence on the face of the world has been climate. Climate is the cauldron in which the makings of all geological changes brew. Nothing in the natural world forms or grows without being affected by weather. Indeed, it is climate that dictates the pattern of life on the surface of this planet.

The Rocky Mountains are famous for their diversity of weather, not just seasonally, but from day to day and hour to hour. Old-timers are likely to advise newcomers who complain of the weather, "If you don't like it – wait five minutes!" Those of us who habitually climb in the high country know something of its amazingly erratic weather. How many times have we climbed a pass on a fine day to run head on into a violent storm at the summit? More than once I have huddled in the lee of a rock outcrop or stunted tree above timberline with my back to the wind and the snow flying so thick that visibility was almost zero. Crouched there I have wondered how anyone could be so foolish as to leave camp without adequate clothing, only to have the sun shine so warm shortly after that my jacket went into my rucksack within the hour.

Observing for the first time the massive bulk of a great peak thrust high against white clouds running on the breeze across a summer sky, you may assume that nothing short of an earthquake could change its features. But take a closer look at the great talus fans, spread in inverted V's, at the foot of the cliffs. Better yet, camp at timberline just beyond the scattering of boulders at the base of such a fan below a cliff perhaps two thousand feet high. Then you will become aware of the sound and movement of mountains – not just the wind roaring and sighing among the rock battlements high overhead, or the soft cadence of falling water where streams play and plunge – but the cacophony of rocks falling onto the scree slope behind your tent. You will find yourself wakened at night by the sudden cannon shot of a boulder sprung from its bed by the pressure of expansion or contraction as the cliff face undergoes a temperature change – a sudden great boom followed by a second cracking report as the boulder strikes a projection of the cliff further down. The rock, in one piece when it started, may be reduced to fragments by the time it reaches the top of the talus rubble pile at the foot of the cliff. There will be a final rattling of stones as they come to rest and then silence again.

Every hour of the day and night during spring, summer and fall, a mountain is continuously shedding loose rock, sometimes with noisy cannonades accompanied by billowing clouds of dust, but usually in more subtle fashion. In winter one chooses his routes of travel and campsites with much greater care, for then the mountains' stress can initiate avalanches, thousands of tons of snow thundering down the slopes and scarring the slopes with their trails.

Regardless of the season there is the constant sight and sound of change, the slow and imperceptible smoothing of the rugged features of the high country. To the uninitiated, it may be frightening at times, but to the old mountain man it is as familiar as the sight of water dripping from the eaves of his cabin or the sound of the kettle on his fire.

Erosion is not without its violent aspects. Most of us who live in southeast British Columbia or southwest Alberta will remember the June storm of 1964, when the normal went into the discard and we found ourselves in the midst of a veritable typhoon more akin to the China Sea. Fifteen inches of warm rain fell on a heavy blanket of snow still covering the mountains. At the height of the storm, when the land was saturated with water, a sudden wind roared in from the northeast. Its velocity, coupled with the great weight of the water it was carrying, hit the standing timber from a direction exactly opposite to the normal prevailing winds. The trees were not rooted to withstand such an onslaught and they went down like dominoes, one falling against another, until in places not a single trunk was left upright. How many moose and other animals perished in this storm there is no way of knowing, but casualties must have been considerable. Not only was the falling timber a hazard, but the accompanying floods were lethal.

One approached the familiar mountain creeks with care to observe the rivers they had become – boiling torrents full of floating timber and rolling boulders. Falls that were normally translucent veils of white water had turned an ugly yellow with silt, spewing boulders into the narrow confines of the canyons. Farther down the lakes and rivers were thick with mud and high over their banks. Nothing to equal this berserk display of nature's power had happened in this area for hundreds of years.

Now, ten years after that storm, nature is covering the scars. Plants are growing to replace those that were covered by sand and gravel; the fallen timber, hidden by a thick growth of willows, berry brush and seedling evergreens, is beginning to rot. The forest regenerates itself and the mountains look down, changed a little in places. But unless one experienced the storm it would be difficult to see and understand the differences.

We have long been conditioned by the forest management people to think of fire as being the most serious threat to our forests. Yet Douglas fir, western larch and yellow pine all have thick, flame resistant bark and require periodic grass and brush fires to control the undergrowth beneath them. Overprotection allows the scrub to grow dangerously high; when a fire does catch and takes off across the country, the flames can reach up into the crowns of the big timber, killing everything. Furthermore, if fire does not make its natural and periodic clean-up, the forage cover beneath the trees is blanketed from the sun and becomes thin, ultimately failing to support the big game populations.

Many of the valleys and ridges in our national parks and forest reserves have been so rigidly protected that normal wintering ranges of the various species of browsers and grazers have been seriously reduced. The timber growth is so thick and widespread that forest fire is very difficult to check when it does get going. In short, the whole ecological system of a mountain area is upset with far-reaching and undesirable consequences.

True, the leftover of a forest fire is a blackened, lifeless, ugly mess with the tall, dead spikes of what were once living trees standing like wooden grave markers in memory of verdant green timber. But soon these bleach out and begin to fall. Seeds that have been lying dormant for perhaps a hundred years or more feel the warm fingers of the sun and begin to sprout. A thick and varied carpet of new growth covers the ground and the herds return to graze in an abundance of feed. It is nature's recycling process at work – a sort of regeneration wrought by climate and one of several ways in which the soil is enriched.

It is the soil that accounts for the presence of the grand bull elk on yonder green slope. Soil is the mother of the magnificent trees standing tall and dignified by the edge of the river. It is the good earth here that supports grass – a most vital and essential species of plants which makes life possible for a multitude of warm-blooded creatures, including man. On the great plains we are aware of the soil, but in the mountains we can see it in the making.

Almost imperceptibly, the climate chews away at the solid rock of the great peaks, lowering them with slow determination, piece by piece, and further weathering and reducing these pieces to dust. The sun and rain then work their powerful sorcery and life teams on the magic carpet thus created.

It is the fluctuating temperatures of the seasons that motivate wildlife migration. Some of these movements cover only short distances, perhaps a drifting of animals a few miles between high, timberline summer pastures and the lower, wind-swept wintering grounds. Such migrations do not usually involve herds of big game but rather smaller groups sifting their way through the scenery so subtly as to be almost unnoticeable.

Bird migrations involve far greater distances. Early one summer our party was camped for a week close by a mountain stream while on a pack train trip. Our cook wore brightly coloured shirts and every morning as he busied himself with breakfast chores a male rufus humming bird would come buzzing up to him, apparently fascinated by the dazzling hue of his apparel. During every spare moment for two days I searched up and down the stream for the nest and finally discovered it in plain sight on a spruce bough overhanging the creek within six feet of where we dipped our water bucket. It was so perfectly camouflaged, I spotted the beak and shining eye of the female sitting on her eggs before realizing I was looking at her nest.

I rode through that camp again in late August to find the nest empty and the hummingbirds nowhere to be seen. No doubt they were on their way towards Central America or even northern South America for the winter. The following July we camped there again and I found an occupied hummingbird nest within a few yards of the location of the one discovered previously. Although there was no sure way to prove it, I strongly suspected they were the same pair back from a round trip of perhaps eight thousand miles, setting up house again within three miles of the crest of the continental divide. What a salutary example of the endurance of a tiny bird – the smallest of them all – and the influence of the sun.

In the fall, when the peaks are showing their first sprinkling of early snow and the timberline larch groves are painted a brilliant gold, we see the first flocks of songbirds, followed by the wildfowl – ducks, geese, swans and various divers – heading south on their way across the mountains towards their wintering grounds in the southern United States.

Among these the common loon is a contributor to the mountain scene. We tend to think of loons as birds of the lonesome spruce-fringed lakes of the far North, but they also nest in the lakes and marshy sloughs of the lower valleys of the Rockies. Their calls are hauntingly beautiful, truly the music of the wilderness.

Apart from the influence of the seasons, the wild ones are sensitive to changes of barometric pressure. If one learns to read their behaviour in such circumstances it is possible to forecast the weather. One fine August morning last summer, two companions and I were climbing the folded slopes near the head of Bighorn Creek in Banff National Park. It was bright and clear with a few cumulus clouds drifting over the peaks across the Cascade Valley. We saw elk in small bunches here and there on the slopes around us. Directly west of us, on the front of a big open ridge beyond the Cascade River, a herd of about a hundred bulls loafed in the sun. By noon an unexpectedly cold wind was blowing and a hard shower drove us down from the high country and back to camp.

It drizzled on and off all afternoon with fog hanging low over the floor of the picturesque valley where our tents were pitched. That evening, while we cooked supper on an open fire in the lee of some spruces close to the creek, we saw a group of twenty-seven elk come down out of the fog onto the slope behind camp. As we watched they began to play, chasing each other back and forth and occasionally rearing straight up to paw at one another. My two young friends were delighted by the sight, but I had forebodings.

"If it were any other time of year but the thirteenth of August," I told them, "I would guess we are in for one hell of a snowstorm!"

Sure enough, we woke next morning to find our tents sagging under the weight of heavy, wet snow and big flakes flying on the wind. Huddled in our ponchos we ate our breakfast around an inadequate fire and chuckled at the sight of wildflowers blooming in the midst of this unseasonal precipitation. The elk had known what was coming and were working to raise their body heat a little in anticipation of it. It snowed continuously for thirty-six hours, for the most part melting as it fell. When the sun came out at noon on the second day, our discomfort was rewarded by the view of glistening timber and the peaks across the valley shining in white blankets.

Where the Mountain Valleys Wander

Until the first white men came to explore the Rocky Mountains, searching for the passes which would encourage the development of the fur trade on the west slope of the continental divide, there was very little inter-mountain travel by man. Prior to the Indians' acquisition of horses, it is doubtful if enough of them crossed the Canadian Rockies to establish the faintest of trails. Even after they became mounted nomads, they were not much inclined towards long journeys in the high country where the buffalo did not penetrate beyond the bigger valleys and where the few moose, elk, deer, mountain sheep and goats offered nothing but hard work in exchange for a mediocre supply of meat. The foreboding peaks with their snowfields and glaciers were particularly uninviting to those Indians who held them in superstition and fear. The narrow valleys leading over the passes were choked with deadfall timber and the swift, icy rivers were a terror. The mighty warrior of the plains hesitated when confronted by a mountain river full of boulders and laced with white water. When it came to bathing, he understandably preferred the traditional steam bath, contrived by pouring water over red hot sacred stones under a canopy of robes supported by a framework of willows.

The North Kootenay, Middle Kootenay and South Kootenay passes, just a few miles north of the forty-ninth parallel, were the most frequently used east-west thoroughfares. Of these, the South Kootenay Pass was the most heavily travelled. The terraced trails, gouged by the hoofs of Indian ponies, are still visible there on both sides of the divide. Unlike the white men that would follow with pack trains in later years, the Indians did not have the means of cutting switchbacks on an easier grade, so they just pushed their horses straight over the height of land, letting the animals pick the line of least resistance along the shortest possible route.

When the Kootenay Indians were defeated by the Blackfoot on the plains east of the Rockies, they migrated west and established themselves along the valley of the river that still carries their name in southeast British Columbia. The Rockies proved to be an effective defence barrier, for apart from a smattering of small raiding parties, the Blackfoot never bothered them there. Occasionally the Kootenays crossed the passes, returning to the buffalo country for a hunt or a raid for horses, but they offered no serious challenge to their old enemies.

In the summer of 1755, Anthony Henday, a fur trader and explorer in the employ of the Hudson's Bay Company, climbed to the top of a butte a few miles north of Calgary and saw the long battlements of the Rockies cleaving the sky seventy miles to the west.

Like his contemporaries, Henday was a product of natural selection and his environment, for a boy had to be a perfect physical specimen and lucky besides to grow to maturity and be chosen for such a life in those days. No doubt when Henday stood on the hilltop looking at the Rockies he was about as tough as a man can become, for he had been living on berries, pemmican and buffalo meat for a long time and had covered many hundreds of miles on foot and on horseback during this westward journey. Just as likely his keen eyes lit up with a desire to push on and discover what lay beyond "the shining mountains," but he was a long way from base. His Cree guides knew nothing of the mountains and probably made no secret of their lack of interest in improving their knowledge. He turned back, carrying the distinction of being the first white man to have seen the Canadian Rockies.

But he had broken a trail and eighty-seven years later, Sir George Simpson, governor of the same company, travelled by pack train up the Bow River and discovered the magnificence of the valley, couched between towering peaks, that is now the site of Banff. Simpson was a restless man of incredible energy, travelling like a wolverine with its tail on fire. In a short time he found two significant passes, later named Simpson and Vermilion, besides being the first man, white or red, to see and record many of the mountain splendours between them.

Although the mountain strongholds may have seemed impregnable, they were being probed here and there by a few adventurous explorers bent on expanding the fur trade. In 1787 David Thompson arrived on the scene leading a small mounted party of five men. Only seventeen years old, he was a trusted and highly respected employee of the Hudson's Bay Company – a young man who was to carve a lasting niche for himself in western history. He caught his first glimpse of the Rockies from a spot not far from Henday's vantage point, and though he may not have realized it then, fate decreed that he would spend the better part of his life journeying back and forth between the Alberta plains and the Pacific coast.

In 1797 he joined the Nor'westers, the highly competitive rival fur trading company that was bent on cornering the trade west of the Rockies. But it would be twenty-one years before David Thompson made his first major moves towards locating the passes that would open a route to the Columbia River drainage.

One day in early May of 1808, he led a string of horses up the Saskatchewan River into the Rockies. He was accompanied by his wife Charlotte, a comely and competent Métis woman, and their three small children. Somewhere not far from the bridge where the Banff-Jasper Highway now crosses the river, he camped to wait for the snow to melt, allowing his pack train to climb a branch valley leading towards the summit of the divide. It must have been an early spring, for he was held up only two weeks. In the meantime his men brought up the necessary supplies and equipment by freight canoe and they sorted out the loads for the horses. On June 25 they broke camp, packed the horses and moved out towards the summit. That night they camped where the streams flowed in two directions out of the melting snowdrifts – part of it heading east to Hudson Bay and the rest pouring down to the west and the Pacific. Thompson had found what was later to be known as Howse Pass and from this vantage point he gazed westwardly across ranges of mountains, wave on wave, stretching into the pale blue distance. Somewhere out there was the Columbia, the river-road to the Pacific Ocean.

With his axemen in the lead he trailed down a creek for several days to a place where it joined a larger river flowing north. Thompson had read Captain Vancouver's journal of his explorations of the Columbia near its mouth and knew that the river he sought ran south. It was to be several years before he realized he had indeed found the mighty Columbia near its meandering source.

The trails of men and most wildlife gravitate to the valleys in mountain country. The rivers point the way to the passes between the peaks and also provide a waterway for canoes. In 1793-4 Alexander Mackenzie took an expedition across North America over a route much longer and more difficult than that followed by the American Lewis and Clark expedition. Mackenzie used canoes all the way to the Pacific by way of the Peace, over the summit at the head of the Parsnip and down the Fraser.

David Thompson employed both canoes and horses in his extensive exploration of interior British Columbia. By whatever means he travelled, he stuck to the valleys winding between mountains. It is doubtful if he ever saw a more beautiful valley than that of the upper Saskatchewan as he blazed a trail to the top of Howse Pass.

I have seen it in early summer when the flower-strewn meadows flanking the river on both sides are lush with grass waving in the wind. Here the valley is nearly a mile wide, affording vistas of the great peaks to the west, their shoulders draped with blue ice and sparkling white snow. Flowing down out of the upper valley the river winds past Whirlpool Point, spreading itself in several channels across wide gravel bars, and then gathering itself into one stream again. At high water time it is a mean river to cross with horses, for the channels are devious with shifting gravel. Opaque with glacier silt the river bottom is hidden, and what might be a passable ford today may be deep enough to swim in tomorrow. At such times it is much more enjoyable to travel along it than to cross it, an observation that applies to most mountain rivers of any size.

David Thompson and his contemporaries were awe-struck by the magnificence and beauty of their surroundings. But none could have dreamed of the changes to follow in the next century or imagined the numbers of people that would be following their trails by the year 1975.

Thompson and his companions had seen the plains east of the mountains alive with game of all kinds. Yet when they penetrated the Rockies they sometimes went hungry, for in the timber of the narrow valleys their progress was noisy and the deer, elk and moose made themselves scarce. Nothing is more likely to disturb wildlife than the sound of an axe biting into a hard log, especially if it echoes off overhanging cliffs. In some of the valleys along the east slope in the southern Canadian Rockies a few buffalo were found on occasion, but they were rare.

Nevertheless buffalo bones have been found on the Saskatchewan, Bow, Oldman and Waterton watersheds well into the mountains. I once dug a cow buffalo skull out of a little swamp at the head of the northwest branch of the Oldman River within a mile of the continental divide. Another time I found the remnants of a bull skeleton at the head of a tributary of the Waterton.

Big game frequents the bottoms of the larger mountain valleys in late fall, winter and early spring, which is the likely explanation for the fact that early exploration parties sometimes went short of food. As soon as the days warm and the slopes begin to turn green, the herds begin to climb up to the high ridges and basins near and above timberline where temperatures are cooler and where they can escape from flies and mosquitoes.

The trappers that rambled the mountain country following the establishment of the fur trade varied their diet with the meat of bighorns and mountain goats. By 1880 the buffalo were gone from the plains and the starving Indians along with early settlers soon decimated the other game. Conservation laws and the formation of the western mountain parks came in time to save what was left.

By 1890 there was a new kind of enterprise starting up in the Rockies. It was the beginning of the era of guides and outfitters. The railroads had been pushed through the Yellowhead, Kicking Horse and Crowsnest passes, linking eastern Canada with the west coast. Conquering the Rockies with iron roads had been difficult and tremendously expensive. Realizing the potential of the mountains' scenic grandeur, the railroad directors persuaded the government in Ottawa to establish Jasper and Banff national parks. They then set about to promote tourist travel and soon people from all over the world were responding. Passengers for the railroads meant profits, thus the early development of the parks was prompted by anything but altruistic motives. Still it was a fortunate development that would be utterly impossible today.

In 1910 Waterton Lakes Park was established in the extreme southwest corner of Alberta, thanks to the insistent demands made by J. G. "Kootenai" Brown and the help of some of his influential friends. Astute enough to realize that their best chance lay in riding the coattails of popular demand further north, they wrote many letters to the ministers in Ottawa extolling the beauties of this mountain country. Kootenai Brown knew it well, for he had come to this region to settle in 1878, and was a well-known hunter and guide. Some of his letters to Ottawa had been illustrated with photographs taken by F. H. Bert Riggall, who had a ranch on Cottonwood Creek. Riggall was opening a guiding and outfitting business and was an artist with his camera. The survey of the park's boundary was ultimately carried out by H. R. MacMillan, official government surveyor at the time, who was later to found the largest privately owned lumber company in the world.

In Banff and Jasper such men as Jim Brewster, Bill Peyto and Jimmy Simpson were cutting trails up the remote valleys where the sound of an axe had never been heard before, and guiding their pack trains into areas of breathtaking beauty. Wealthy aristocracy from Europe and the United States was attracted by this region of natural wonders. Famous climbers familiar with the European Alps came to conquer the high peaks. People from every walk of life joined in the parade to see the new national parks.

The outfitters who supplied the horse transportation for these sight-seers were a breed unto themselves; to a man, they were a physically hardy, enterprising and picturesque lot. When it came to handling horses and managing sizable parties of green tourists in wild mountain country, they had no equal. Some of the big trail rides organized by the Brewsters in Banff involved as many as four hundred horses – a kind of organized nightmare in some respects, but offering a service that the ordinary man could afford.

Most of the outfitters handled much smaller parties of wealthier patrons who could pay for a very specialized kind of service. These were deluxe expeditions of up to a month's duration, serving excellent meals on the trail and providing the finest equipment. Sometimes the equipment even included rubber bathtubs so that milady from London or Paris, attended by her personal maid, could enjoy her morning bath. The maids sometimes proved vulnerable to their new environment and became so entranced with the country and the blandishments of colourful wranglers and guides that they defected, eventually to marry and to adopt this new land as their own.

The society of the mountains is classless to a large extent, and any scion of aristocracy who attempted to treat an outfitter's crew with less than respect soon discovered that this was a sure way to have his tea served with salt. Life on the wilderness trails is a great leveller, where people are judged by their true characters rather than by the size of their bank accounts. For the most part, the guests adapted quickly and proceeded to enjoy a unique wilderness adventure in the company of expert and friendly mountain men. It was not unusual for members of the titled nobility of Europe or the princes of industry to form lasting friendships with their hosts, friendships that lasted through generations of their respective families.

Some of the outfitters went to great lengths to offer extra attractions.

To provide the ultimate in experience and skill, Swiss guides were imported to take charge of the many climbing parties assaulting the unclimbed peaks. Some of the world's top climbers brought their personal guides with them. Most of the outfitters themselves were expert hunting guides, able to lead their sporting patrons in successful pursuit of fine trophies from the game herds outside the parks.

While hunting was a part of their business, the Rocky Mountain outfitters were primarily concerned with summer sight-seeing and sport fishing parties. Many of the mountain streams abounded with trout.

Bert Riggall, whose pack train trails reached north from Waterton Lakes across the headwaters of the Oldman and Highwood rivers to the foot of the Kananaskis Range, and west to the North Fork of the Flathead River in British Columbia, was no exception. He was a noted big game guide who knew the habits of the bighorn from birth to death. While several bighorn trophies taken by his clients are still listed in the record book, perhaps he is best remembered for the service provided to family parties on his summer pack trains in the Rockies.

A voracious reader with an encyclopedic mind, Riggall could entertainingly explain the many fascinating details of alpine flora and fauna, geography and geology. He provided much more than just good trail service; his guests were treated to a concentrated course in natural history which had great impact on his students, particularly the youngsters. He was a kindly and quiet man who managed his pack outfit with the firm hand of a ship's captain. While his word was law on the trail, he rarely raised his voice in anger or exasperation, and he possessed a keen sense of humour. Many of the people who took these wilderness trips with him returned again and again through several generations, some beginning at a very early age and barely old enough to ride a gentle horse.

Having worked with him for years, first as a sort of apprentice and then as a partner, I regarded him as a close friend. For me it was a rare and rewarding opportunity to acquire some lasting understanding of the mountains and the life therein, knowledge that served me well in later years.

Memory takes me back to a day when we pitched camp up on the headwaters of the Oldman in a spot that was truly lovely. There were a dozen people in the party – three generations of the same family. After supper we gathered around a small fire in an Indian tepee while everyone took a turn contributing to the evening's entertainment. It was not unlike a family reunion, for these folks were old friends. After everybody had gone to their respective bed tents for the night and Bert and I were preparing to get into our sleeping robes, I remarked that it was quite a life we enjoyed, making a living at having so much fun.

"They are wonderful people," I said finally.

Bert looked at me across the dying embers of the fire, his eyes twinkling. "They should be," he said. "We raised 'em!"

He wasn't stretching the truth as much as it might appear, for we guided four generations of that family over a period of some fifty years. I remember Bert Riggall with warm affection, a man of rare eloquence, wisdom and wit.

But the golden years of the outfitter did not last. Following the low ebb of World War II there was a brief upsurge that approached the old days, but the smell of change was in the wind. No longer did the wilderness country stretch across unlimited miles. The uncaring bulldozer blades of industry were opening the country to oil and mineral exploration as well as timber exploitation until there was barely a valley left outside the parks where one could not drive on wheels. Even the parks were not immune to the spell of road building. A few years previous mountain visitors did not think they had arrived until they had taken a wilderness trail trip on horseback. Now the fashion is to streak through the parks for two or three days, and then boast of having "done" such-and-such an area. The old-time outfitter's rejoinder is to spit in the grass with such vitriolic disgust that the grass never grows there again!

Many people have faith in the outdated advertising of the national parks, yet this advertising constitutes an embarrassment. Traffic jams miles long at the park entrances have become commonplace. On holiday weekends accommodation becomes so scarce that one could rent out a stall in a horse stable, as some of us have done, in order to get people in out of the rain.

Because park regulations restrict the use of horses, the back country traveller now goes afoot. The backpacker carries a minimum of specialized equipment and freeze-dried food balanced on a light aluminum packframe, the modern equivalent of the pack horse. The mountain traveller's range of activity is limited by his or her physical stamina and the amount that can be carried. In spite of these limitations, restrictions not experienced even by the earliest explorers who at least had horses, the numbers of people using the back country trails are legion and growing.

One evening last summer I walked into one of the government specified camps fifty odd miles up the Snake Indian River in northern Jasper Park. It had been a long, hot day. My load weighed close to fifty-five pounds, my feet were hurting and I was mighty glad to throw down my pack for the night. But there was scarcely room to pitch my tent in the crowded campground, for at least forty people were there ahead of me though it was only 5:30 in the afternoon.

Most of these people were on their way up the Snake Indian River past Little Heaven and over the pass heading down to Twin Trees Lake. From there they would go down to the Smokey River and then up to the pass at the foot of Mount Robson, over to Berg Lake and from there to the highway. The journey involved a hundred miles of foot travel through rugged country where the trails are worn deep by many boots and the camps bare of a single blade of grass, all vegetation wiped out by the sheer weight of people. Four hundred hikers made the trip last year and more will do so next summer.

Later in the evening I walked out beyond the edge of the campsite to a low bank by a sleepy little creek flowing down to the Snake Indian from the north between folded, timber-clad hills. Looking west I could see the rugged ramparts of the Great Divide standing tall against the sky. Off to the south lightning was flashing around the base of a towering thunderhead, but the storm was so far away there was no sound of thunder. It was very quiet except for a sighing breeze and the rippling sounds of the creek.

Somewhere behind me a girl laughed and then lifted her voice in song, accompanied by a guitar. She was improvising a ballad about the mountains, the roar of river rapids, the winding trail through spires of spruce trees, the rain and the hot sun. She sang of the wilderness and its peaceful beauty, her voice rising full and clear and then carried away by the breeze. Had some musician sung in the camps of Thompson or Mackenzie, inspired by the power of big rivers, by the sight of the great peaks flanking the canyons?

To them it had been utterly wild. When I first travelled the old pack train trails fifty years ago, we might not have seen another party of travellers in a month. Now I realized that to this girl and the rest of the people here in camp, crowded though it was, it was still supreme wilderness in all its raw, pristine beauty.

The ultimate quality of wilderness is no doubt influenced by personal experience and comparison with the places from which we come. The Indians had once appreciated this spot – in my off-trail ramblings I found signs of their camps and the faint evidence of a grave; they had called this wilderness home and changed it not at all. The early explorers fought with it to stay alive. Today we see this land as something to be preserved, but useful only if we use it, and by degrees we change it into something else. We have created the parks to ensure the survival of natural beauty for all time. Obviously a great many of us love these wilderness regions of the Rockies but will we love them to death?

I wondered, and the girl's song did not say.

31 The Giant Steps waterfall on Paradise Creek in the valley between Ten Peaks and Lake Louise.

32 Waterfalls are beyond number in the Rockies and many, like this one in a remote part of Banff National Park, are unnamed. Some thunder and roar with smashing force in their descents; others make gentle music amid lacy veils.

33 Johnston Canyon in Banff National Park is a typical example of water-eroded rock. Prior to the ice ages the valleys of the Rockies were similarly narrow and steep-walled.

34 Few things are more satisfying to the aesthetic soul of a wilderness wanderer than the sight and sound of pure water falling from the flank of a mountain. This waterfall is located not far from Banff townsite.

35 Wapta Falls on the Kicking Horse River is the largest waterfall in Yoho Park.

36 Caught in a round depression, rocks whirled by fast flowing water sculpted this bird's nest form beside a small creek that flows into Berg Lake.

37 The carving force of water is totally unpredictable, powerful and surprisingly artistic. This scene was photographed above Berg Lake.

38 Sometimes a waterfall, however beautiful, can be a deadly trap. This hidden falls in Waterton Lakes National Park is heavily camouflaged at its top by brush and could be a pitfall for animals – and men – coming downstream from above.

39 The Alexandra River is a typical braided glacial stream. Such streams pour down from the glaciers and deposit silt on the lower valley floors, thus creating a fertile bed for vegetation.

40 A moth struggles on the surface of a still pool making a pattern of concentric circles.

41 Maligne Lake in Jasper National Park has been photographed countless times yet no two pictures are the same. The ever-changing patterns of light and

season on mountains and water offer a multitude of effects.

42 Industrious beavers often change the scenes in the Rockies as the aspen and cottonwood stumps attest in this view of Mount Rundle.

43 Meltwater running down from the glacier into Peyto Lake is slowly but surely filling it with silt.

44 An early September snowfall mantles the slopes in sharp contrast to the deep blue of Kiwetinok Lake, far above timberline at the head of Little Yoho Valley.

45 Wildflower Creek from Pulsatilla Pass, which derives its name from pulsatilla, the old name for mountain avens, a common alpine flower. The mountain on the left is Mount Avens.

46 Bighorn sheep beautifully outlined against a vista of lakes and mountains in Banff National Park overlooking Lake Minnewanka.

47 The first harbingers of spring in the Rockies are the pussy willow blooms. Male flowers often exhibit pink stamens tipped with yellow pollen.

48 Over fifty kinds of mushrooms grow on the forest floors in the Rockies – most of them edible. They come in a wide variety of size, exotic shape and colour. Pine squirrels will gather them, hang them on tree branches to dry, and store them for the winter.

49 Mushrooms grow best in damp places like this spot among green horsetail and rotting logs.

50 The Canada violet or wood violet lifts its impish face in June and July in the cool, moist woods of the Rockies.

51 Forest fires strike terror in the hearts of all wild things. Awesome yet destructive, naturally caused fires are part of nature's regeneration cycle.

52 While careless people are responsible for some forest fires, most often it is lightning strikes that set them off. First one tree flames, then another and still another, until a conflagration rages that may wipe out miles of timber in a matter of hours.

53 What remains is a blackened landscape soon made green again by fireweed, grass and brush. Seedling trees will begin to show and the area will slowly restore itself till once more tall timber shades the ground.

54 Mountain ash berries lend a brilliant splash of colour. Bears will eat them occasionally, but they are tough and astringent to the taste.

55 Devil's club, growing on the forest floor beneath giant cedars, is one of nature's most diabolical botanical creations. It is covered with poisonous thorns, even to the backs of the leaves, and woe to any man who travels too far through such a tangle without adequate protection.

56 In contrast to the rain forest home of the devil's club are the grass slopes between stringers of timber common to the east slope of the Rockies.

57 A newborn mule deer fawn lies still as a bronze statue, camouflaged against prying eyes by its dappled coat.

58 When mountains stand on their heads – a reflection of the Ramparts in a pool near Amethyst Lakes in Jasper National Park.

59 Looking south to the Amethyst Lakes and Tonquin Valley from Vista Peak in Jasper National Park. The mountains on the distant skyline are the rugged setting of the Columbia Icefield.

60 Chak Peak near Portal Pass lifts its head against heavy clouds after a summer snowstorm.

61 A vista of mountains, looking north across the hairpin bends of the Athabasca River in Jasper National Park.

62 The mountain peaks rake the bottoms of the clouds overlooking the headwaters of the Smokey River not far from the continental divide.

63 No vagrant breeze disturbs this mirror reflection in a backwater along the Athabasca River. From left to right: Mount Christie, Brussels Peak and Mount Fryatt.

64 The Bow River runs free of its winter shackles of snow and ice in early spring at the foot of majestic Castle Mountain.

65 The western lily is a brilliant flower common to the foothills along the east slope of the Rockies in early summer.

66 A tiny boreal owl and its prey, a captured vole. This owl commonly nests in tree cavities pecked out by pileated woodpeckers.

67 The most superb climber in the Rockies, the mountain goat spends its life on the cliffs and rock slides. Here it has little to fear from predators and enjoys minimum competition from other ungulates.

68 Mischievous fox pups pause in their play near the mouth of the home den to watch expectantly for the parents to return with the evening meal.

69 It is a rare thing to spot a cougar in the wilds for it is largely nocturnal. It lives exclusively on prey ranging from moose to rabbits and is probably the most efficient killer of all the world's big cats.

70 "Who goes there?" this big grizzly seems to ask, as she rears to full height and peers short-sightedly in an attempt to identify her visitor.

71 The false hellebore displays an interesting design of leaf as it grows rapidly in late spring. Its roots were dried and used as a kind of snuff by the Indians as a cure for head colds.

72 Water and ice-worn rocks bedded in silt form a wilderness mosaic typical of a glacial stream.

73 The stillness is profound after an early autumn snowstorm lays its first promise of winter on the trees and slopes around Lake O'Hara in Yoho National Park.

74 The sensuous forms of fresh fallen snow over boulders flank the spring waters of this mountain stream where its subterranean warmth keeps the frost at bay.

75 A reflection of sun and clouds on the surface of Vermilion Lake is captured by the photographer. By underexposing the water he achieved a galaxy-like image.

31

34

35

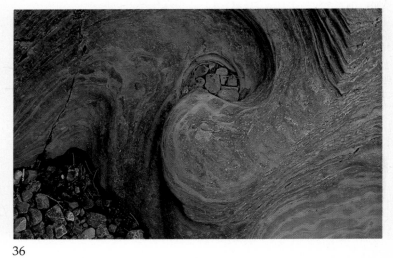

36

37

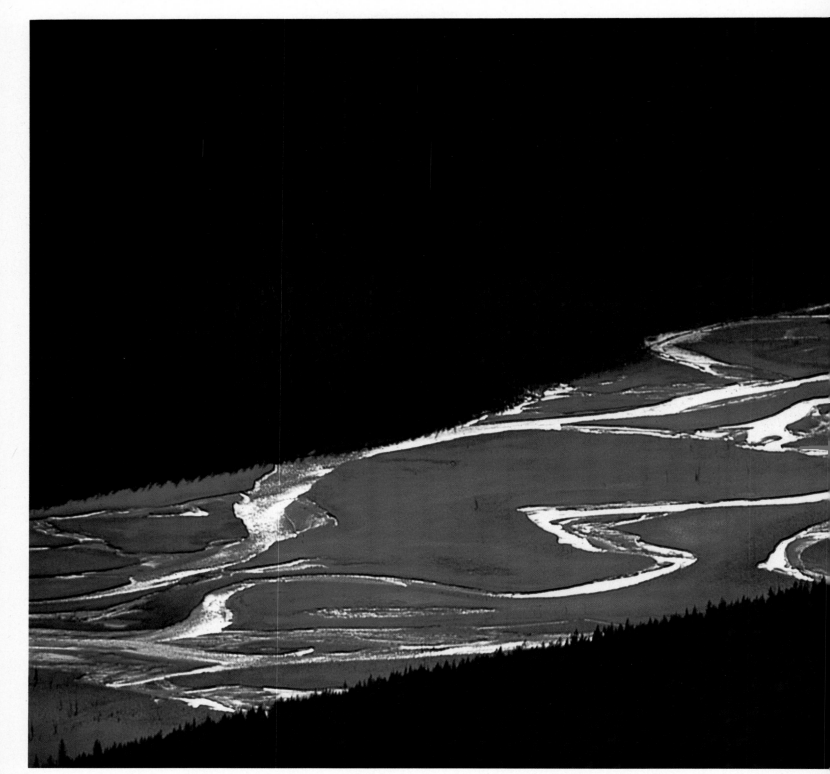

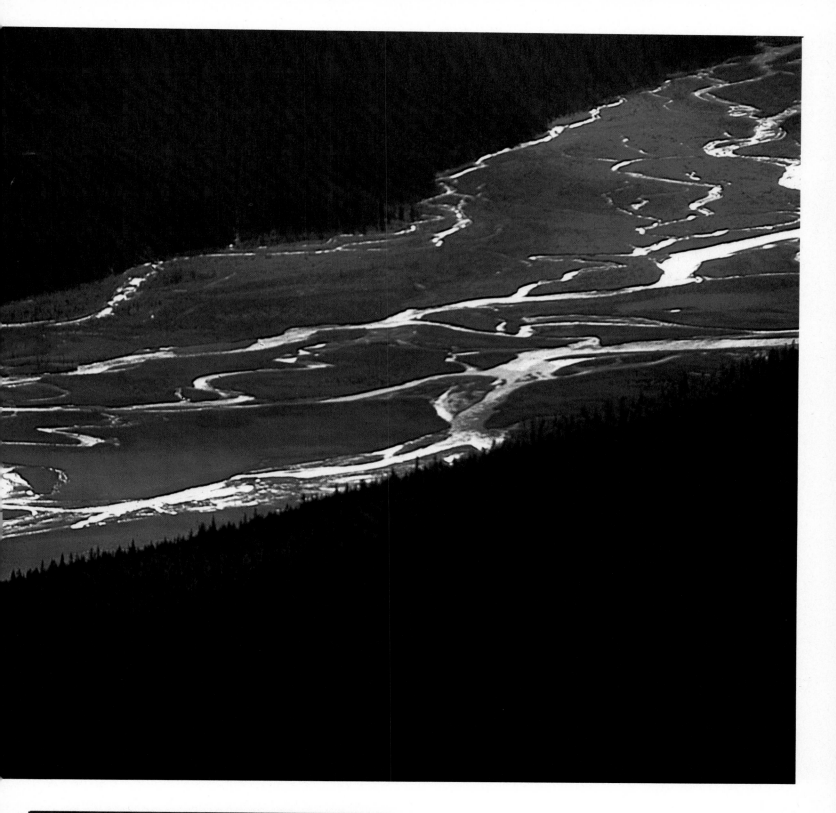

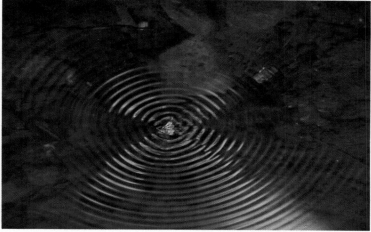

41

42

44

43

46

47

50

51

52

53

54

55

56

57

61

62

63

65

66

67

68

69

70

71

74

75

Where the Beaver Swims

Those white men who first broke trail through the Rockies – Henday, Simpson, Thompson and the rest – were not out simply to satisfy their curiosity or for the exercise. They were pushing hard to open new territory for the fur trade; fine furs were in great demand as garments for milord and lady, and particularly for the manufacture of beaver hats.

The unobtrusive beaver was the key animal in the trade. It was later chosen to be Canada's national symbol largely because of its impact on the history of this country. The efficient network of the fur trade and the keen demand for beaver fur came within a whisker of wiping out the animal. The trail that the old traders followed was that of exploitation without thought for the future – a trail of no return. What they best understood was how to get the most pelts in the shortest possible time, and the trade almost destroyed itself in the process.

The sheer ruggedness and inaccessibility of much of the beaver habitat was the one factor that saved the animal from complete extinction. At the heads of the rivers flowing down off both sides of the Rockies pockets of beaver population remained hidden and unmolested. When conservation laws and the national parks came into being, the beaver once more began to increase and spread out along these streams. When one considers how rapidly the beavers were hunted out over a vast area by relatively few people, and how close we came to losing them forever, one appreciates the sometimes frightening impact that man can make on a natural environment over a very short period of time.

One evening years ago, while camped on the lower reaches of Kishaneena Creek not far north of the international boundary in the southeast corner of British Columbia, I picked up my flyrod and wandered out along the stream to catch some trout for breakfast. My trail took me through a grove of great cottonwoods and smooth-barked aspens standing tall and green among darker spruces. Shoulder high on the north side of some of the larger aspens I noticed some unusual marks. They were circular designs of small black scars about an inch apart – signs left by a trapper years before when he nailed up his beaver pelts flesh side out to dry. I knew the man, though he is now long dead, and unlike many of his kind he was a conservationist, never taking more of the furbearers than the population of his territory could afford.

Proof of his foresight was evident only a few steps away on the bank of the creek: there stood the fresh stump of a giant cottonwood cut down by a hard working pair of beavers over a period of several nights. The stump was three feet in diameter and the trunk lying on the ground beside it was ninety-three feet long. The beavers could handle only the smaller trimmings from its top. They had laboured long for the winter supplies, now sunk in deep water not far from the mouth of their bank den. The pile of chips cut by their sharp teeth lay in a circular arrangement several inches deep all around the stump as further proof of their diligence and determination.

The characteristic style of their cutting prevented an accurate count of the stump's annual rings, nor did I take time to retrieve a sharp axe from my pack and trim the stump on a bevel to allow for a more careful determination of its age. But in view of its size, that cottonwood had to be at least two hundred years old. When Anthony Henday enjoyed his first view of the Rockies, it had likely been a slim tree. I had stood beside its stump and seen jet trails in the sky.

The big tree had been there when the Kootenays rode down through the pass bearing their name, heading west after the fierce Blackfoot had defeated them. The old South Kootenay trail wound through the grove only a few yards away. This tree had felt the vibration of exploding gunpowder, when an old-time trapper had accidentally shot himself with his own set-gun fixed to wipe out a grizzly bear. Its leaves had stirred in a breeze full of the music of the Swiss bells on our pack train many times over the years. What a story it could tell of drama, hardship and good times along the old trail. Much of that story, dated by the annual rings of its growth history, would have been connected with beaver and now two of these industrious rodents had cut it down.

Along the larger streams of the mountains, beavers locate on the edges of the big pools and deeper backwaters. Building dams across river is impossible for them, so they use the natural shelter of slack waters and banks for house and den sites. They do dam up the smaller tributary streams feeding the rivers, sometimes with a continuous step-like series of dams. Such construction can be a problem to the mountain traveller, for the numerous ponds and canals thus formed can be a real hazard.

A couple of my guests and I once scouted a trail through a remote part of the Flathead valley in British Columbia. It was June, when the waters of the creeks and rivers were booming in flood. We had spent most of the day riding through high timberline parks and basins, and after making a circle were back in the vicinity of camp. Along toward evening we came out on top of a hog back ridge on a good trail – a trail that would eventually lead us home by a circuitous route of five or six miles' length. By cutting straight down a creek we could reach camp after a mile and a half's travel. It would mean bushwhacking through thick, second growth lodgepole pine part of the way, always an unknown quantity, but it was hot and we were tired. The temptation overrode my better judgment, and so we headed down the creek.

For the first quarter mile the going was good, but then the valley narrowed for a way and we fought for passage through the pines growing as thick as the hair on a bear's back. We emerged at a flat of willows and aspens, normally easier going; instead, we found ourselves in even greater difficulty. Our horses nearly bogged down in the mud amongst the beaver dams built on a small side creek, and we became trapped in a maze of downed logs left by the beavers. As the old saying goes, we were caught between a rock and a hard place, in a spot midway to our objective. There was no profit in backtracking to the trail. We ended up taking to the creek – virtually a river at this time of year – and wading and swimming our horses downstream. Thanks to strong, fearless mounts we made it without incident and suffered only a thorough soaking. We finally arrived in camp convinced that a shortcut in such wild country can often prove to be the longest way around.

One of my favourite spots in the Rockies is an abandoned channel formed by a river that has cut across one of its own bends, leaving a long oxbow-shaped pond fed by springs and dammed by beavers at both ends. It is an aquatic world unto itself, where trout leap and play as they feed on the rich insect life of the crystal clear water. Willows and scrub birch hang down over the pond affording cover for a host of songbirds. Ducks and a pair of Canada geese habitually nest there. To sit quietly on the bank with a pair of good binoculars is to enjoy a continuous show of all kinds of wildlife. To observe it at its best, one should visit a half hour before sunset on an evening in early summer. Take a comfortable position overlooking as much of the water as possible and be as still as a stone.

My most recent intrusion exploded a pair of mallards off the water along with a lone goose. A few minutes after I settled down, my back resting against a big log, one end of which was submerged in the pond, the ducks came back to land in front of me. The goose passed overhead, heading downstream and talking to itself with low honks – probably the gander of the nesting pair. For a while the mallards sat on the water with their heads up, wary and watchful. Deciding that no immediate danger lurked close by, they began searching for feed below the water's surface.

A muskrat popped up not far away to swim over within a couple of feet of my boot toes, crawl up the submerged end of my back rest and proceed with its toilet. For a few minutes it scratched and combed its fur, then ambled into some lush grass growing on a spit of silt. There it fed for a while, gathering a mouthful of the green stuff, before re-entering the pond and diving from sight. Likely it was taking the feed to its den and a few minutes later it reappeared near the mallards. For a while the muskrat lay on the water without a move, peering at the ducks. It looked like a stick floating on the surface, its tail elevated at a slight angle above the water. Then it dove again and an instant later the drake gave a startled quack and flipped to one side as the muskrat torpedoed him. The ducks hastily paddled away, while the muskrat, seemingly satisfied with his little joke, swam back to shore a few yards from me and began gathering more feed.

As the sun's edge touched the top of the mountain to the west, a robin called from a nearby tree and willow thrushes performed the evening conta-ta. There is no bird song so fitting to a mountain evening than that of willow thrushes, for there is something about their liquid tones drifting down the scale that goes with the cool bowers of willows and aspens and the faint accompaniment of leaves vibrating in soft zephyrs.

As the sun dipped from sight, a stick cracked and my binoculars picked up a patch of black hide showing through a tangle of scrubby birch. My first thought was of bear, but then a huge old grey-muzzled bull moose strode into view and paused for a moment as though contemplating his reflection on the water before wading belly deep into the pond to feed on the aquatic growth on its bottom. Head and velvet-covered antlers completely out of sight under the surface, he nuzzled about for a mouthful of plants, then raised his head to chew while water cascaded off the palms of his growing weapons and ran in streams down the bell under his jaw. He flicked his ears at the sudden slap of a beaver's tail coming down hard on the water from around a bend fifty yards away then ducked his head for more. The beaver paddled up quite close to give him a long hard look as though demanding an explanation for the intrusion. He dove and reappeared squarely in front of me, then swam away down toward the river.

A layer of high cirrus clouds over the mountains had turned shell pink in colour. The feeding moose created wavelets that glinted in reflection of the sunset. Suddenly the bull paused in his chewing to point his ears at something in the timber straight across the pond, his body motionless with an intent concentration that spoke of danger. No twig snapped to give away the presence in the trees; it was the breeze that carried the message to his nose. After a tense pause, the bull abruptly launched himself for shore, leapt up the bank and trotted away. The sudden noise of his departure stilled the bird song momentarily and again there came the flat crack of a beaver, somewhere out of sight, sounding alarm with a trowel tail applied smartly to the water. Whatever had spooked the moose remained hidden and I wondered if it was the big tom cougar that sometimes visited this place.

One night the previous September, after a sudden heavy fall of snow that choked the pond with slush and bent the aspens and willows into a confusion of interlaced saplings and branches, the moon had come out to light up the scene almost as bright as day. Up on a ridge flanking the valley, a bull elk herded a harem of cows on a bulging shoulder of the hillside among some aspen groves. The whole valley rang with his challenges as he traded threats with two rivals, both lesser animals with light racks and not inclined to carry the argument beyond bugling. But they kept the herd bull busy as they circled around trying to cut out a cow or two for themselves. The cows were hungry, and because of the snow they tended to wander as they searched for feed, a habit that did not ease the big bull's problems. He advertised his displeasure with almost continuous herding accompanied by full-throated bugling.

Up in a grove of spruces roughly a quarter mile above the elk a shadow stirred, then resolved itself into a tom cougar that walked out into the moonlight alongside a log and stood with ears cocked in the direction of the elk. With head held low he crossed a meadow slope moving towards the sound of the animals below. Almost eight feet from nose to tip of tail, he was a giant of his kind and his belly was growling with hunger. The damp breeze filled his nostrils with the musky smell of elk and he padded closer, a smooth-moving specialty of nature that animated menace with every roll of the muscles under his tawny hide. With a casualness that was utter deception, he mounted a rock outcrop and flattened out at the sudden racket of antlers on a dead tree. One second he was pure poetry of motion and the next, perfectly still. Not a hair of him moved as he lay like a piece of the solid stone under him, eyes fixed on the scene below.

For many minutes the cougar remained frozen on top of the outcrop while elk moved in and beyond a strip of snow-draped aspens. Finally one of the young bulls saw his chance and came streaking up the slope from below while the herdmaster was busy with the other rival on the far side of the cows. With a deft twist of his shoulders, he pivoted to cut out a fat two-year-old cow, driving her through the aspens and out onto the open slope. The cougar, with long tail held high, launched himself in the flying leap that brought him down squarely on the cow's back. Setting his claws into warm, yielding skin, his jaws reached for the back of her neck. She bucked under him, snorting with a sharp high sound of escaping breath as she whirled to leap downhill. The cow's blind rush propelled her head-on into an aspen with such force that a three-inch trunk broke off square four feet from the ground. The sudden jolt almost dislodged the cat, but the cow fell and before she could more than kick, sharp teeth met with a crunch in the vertebrae of her neck.

While the cow thrashed in her death throes, the cougar braced himself and hung on, oblivious to the sounds of wildly stampeding elk already fading in the distance. Only when she ceased to move did he let go. After a while he fed on the warm meat and when his belly was full, he partially covered the carcass with snow and forest debris. Then he climbed back up the slope, curled up and slept under the wide-spread branches of a spruce.

Next day I found the remains of the cow and read the story plain as newsprint in the snow.

Six weeks later, the cougar came back and this time stalked and killed four young beaver over a period of a week while the family worked at cutting and dragging in the winter food supply of aspens and willows. Either the parent pair became aware of his presence and exercised more caution or the big cat had his attention drawn elsewhere. In any case they survived to raise another litter of young, one of which was now swimming past me as the first stars came out. Perhaps these would be more fortunate.

Nature's stories are sometimes written in blood, but in their own way even the tragedies are fascinating, for all wild things are either prey or predators, and their patterns of life are inextricable. It has been this way since the dawn of life and it will continue to be this way as long as water runs downhill.

The history of man and natural history have always been bound together even though they are often at war; man's technology and his application of it to the exploitation of his environment have tended to blur the ties that bind him to nature. But we ignore our dependence on the natural world to our peril.

Human history is vital, compelling, interesting – so is natural history, and only with a thorough understanding of both can we fully appreciate the intricate network of their relationship. In the Rockies we often glimpse illustrations of this, where within the space of a few miles and a few thousand feet of elevation we can find evidence of the grossest disregard and contempt for nature. And at the same time nature illuminates its ability to adapt, to develop and to foster life systems of almost endless variety. Nature is at once powerful and rugged yet beautiful and extremely fragile. Only through an appreciation of the interwoven patterns of the species can future generations hope to enjoy its many rewarding features.

Man has proved his intelligence in the development of a complex technology. Why not apply it in such a manner that we can benefit from natural resources and at the same time ensure their conservation and preservation to the maximum? It can be done; perhaps it must be done to ensure our survival.

Early one day last fall, on the upper reaches of the Athabasca River, I left my car, shouldered a light pack containing lunch and camera equipment and headed straight up a mountain slope to the east of the river. Within twenty steps of the highway I was in a trackless wilderness amongst thick, heavy forest that had seen no fire for at least a century and a half. My objective was a high, south facing timberline basin, a steeply pitched green pasture exposed to the sun where I had spotted seventeen goats the evening before – all billies in heavy October coats complete with flowing beards and pantaloons. I hoped to get within camera range for some pictures, but to do so would require some prolonged effort, for it was steep country and the going was rough through groves of pine and spruce timber, copiously strewn with deadfalls. The farther I went the steeper it became until I was climbing as well as crawling over logs. But with three months of mountain travel behind me, my muscles were toned to a point where the exertion was enjoyable.

Just the same it was work, lifting every pound of body and pack several inches in elevation with each step. By noon I was close to timberline at least three thousand feet above my starting place and ready to sit down on top of a rock ledge for a lunch of cheese, sausage, biscuits and chocolate. Below me the river gleamed like silver in the sun as it wound down the valley at the foot of a long line of the tremendous peaks. Hanging glaciers glittered and the bare shoulders of the great crags were dusted with a fresh fall of new snow. Combined with the golden splash of aspens in the low valley, it was an idyllic scene typical of the Rockies in the fall when the air is clear as crystal. But for the road, the mountains and the valley appeared to me almost exactly as David Thompson had seen them and I had the advantage of a camera to record them in a setting as wild and free as had so often been encountered by that stout-hearted explorer.

After lunch I pushed on, climbing around a point overlooking the basin on its south rim. Directly across from me ten of the billies lay sprawled on a mountain meadow, trapped between secondary cliffs at the foot of a steep shoulder. They were not very far away, but still beyond the range of my longest lens.

The basin was more like a gigantic box canyon, very steep at its head and flanks and rimmed with a series of cliffs. There would be nothing gained in trying to cross it, for that meant climbing down a long way and then back up to the level of the goats. The best strategy was to circle around the head of it, under the cliffs. But this posed its problems too, for the north facing slope was covered with an inch of snow and frozen hard. Luckily I found a goat trail at the foot of the cliffs leading in the right direction and proceeded to follow it. At best it was no boulevard and in places it was definitely dangerous. I was wearing good climbing boots but needed an ice axe where the trail thinned and offered barely a toehold. By going slowly and with the utmost care I crossed a very bad stretch at the head of an old avalanche track where a slip would have meant disaster. Finally I reached an easier section that led me past the foot of a falls at the head of the canyon and from there the trail improved on the slope facing the sun.

In the meantime the goats were up and feeding. Four of them had disappeared but six big billies were grazing on a hanging meadow. Slipping through a stringer of scrub timber, I screwed my camera and its 300 mm lens on the tripod and shot a couple of pictures. Then they spotted me; without further preamble they hoisted their short tails straight in the air and walked up a chimney, soon dropping out of sight over a shoulder of the mountain.

Suddenly my legs were tired, my feet hurt and my enthusiasm was akin to a leaky kettle putting out the fire meant to heat it for tea. Sitting there, I recalled the many times when a stalk after goats had ended the same way and I put aside the inclination to wonder at my own sanity. Two miles away as the eagle flies and thousands of feet below I could see my car and envied the raven that was playing in a wind current between. Packing away the camera I headed straight down the canyon.

Climbing a slope when one is fresh is one thing; descending a steep mountain flank at the end of a long day over the roughest kind of footing is quite another. One becomes acutely aware of every step. Paralleling the rim of a twisted gorge overhanging the creek for half a mile, I came out of the timber on top of a cliff about two hundred feet high. Climbing down a cliff that one has come up is relatively easy if there are shelves and a route has been located. This one had some shelves, but they were separated by sheer rock and the footing was an unknown quantity. Good sense said to traverse the rim until I came to a break, but my leg muscles ached at the idea, so I tackled the steep cliff face. The sun was getting low as I eased down over several steep places to reach the midway point. There I was on top of an unbroken vertical pitch about thirty feet high. Scouting north brought me to a place where the ledge pinched out to nothing, so I turned back, wondering if I would be able to beat the dark or if I was looking at the probability of an overnight Siwash camp. It was not a very cheerful prospect, for I realized that I had not seen a single spot all day flat enough to offer any comfort or the assurance of safety.

Then ahead of me along the ledge I saw the tip of a tree sticking up a few feet out of a chimney. It was a slim lodgepole pine growing up from the ledge below and at that moment it suggested a stepladder. Carefully I reached out, pulled it to me and stepped into its branches. My weight held it against the rock face and in a few moments I was down. Now it was a simple matter of walking across country to the car – but little did I know.

When I got down to the comparatively flat ground of the valley floor it was to encounter an awful tangle of blow-down timber. If the trees had all fallen one way it wouldn't have been so bad, but some freak of wind had upset them in a snarl six to eight feet deep, trunks pointing in all directions. By this time I was near the end of my physical rope, well into the middle of the mess, and there was no percentage in trying to back out. Painfully I crawled, scrambled and broke my way through a few feet at a time, until finally the road appeared through the forest. The stars were out by the time I reached the station wagon half a mile away. It had been a long day.

The Rockies are always beautiful, but sometimes their beauty is eclipsed by conditions that are cruel and utterly exhausting. The mountains are full of contrasts; the variety of terrain over relatively short distances can be mind-boggling.

Timberline is the transition zone between the boreal forest and the alpine. It is a place where meadows mingle with the trees in a combination that affords vistas of high lakes and peaks often framed between the green branches of larches and alpine fir trees. The elevation of timberline varies with the latitude, and where treeline is encountered between six and seven thousand feet above sea level at the forty-ninth parallel, it will occur at only two thousand feet up at the British Columbia-Yukon border. Still farther north, where the Rockies slope down to the Arctic Ocean, the only tall trees are found in the bottoms of the lowest valleys a few feet above sea level.

There the biggest tree found on the slopes of the mountains is the arctic willow, rarely more than six inches in height.

At the head of the Prophet River in northeastern British Columbia I once camped in a grove of spruce at timberline. They were jug-butted old trees, the largest being eighteen to twenty inches in diameter. I counted the rings as well as I could on such a tree and estimated its age at seven hundred and fifty years! A timberline larch one and a quarter inches through, cut in a high basin in British Columbia just north of the international boundary, proved to be ninety-three years old. There are a few big ones in the Lynham Basin in Waterton Lakes Park over three feet in diameter and how many years it took them to grow to this size is anybody's guess. Core samplings reveal that these trees are rotten and hollow in the middle, but if some way could be found to age them it is quite likely such trees would rank with the redwoods and bristlecone pines as being among the oldest living things in North America.

In July of last summer we camped near the head of the Oldman River not far from the foot of Beehive Peak. A few minutes' walk put us at timberline on a series of low ridges that led towards Windy Pass. It is well-named, for gales roar through this area regularly, especially in winter, and the twisted contours of the limber pine, alpine firs and larches there bear testimony to the punishment they endure. While the weather was perfect during our visit, I had seen it when one would have had to crawl on hands and knees to get over the pass. Trees over a foot in diameter at the butt have never stood in an upright position, but grow parallel to the ground, sprawling away from the direction of the prevailing wind as though in supplication. I found one over two feet through that was dead and bleached at the butt but that had taken root halfway up the trunk in a pile of drift dirt and its top was still green and growing. How many years its roots had clawed for a living there is no telling, but certainly it must have been hundreds of years. It was a rugged plant, the picture of a tough, wind-tortured existence, yet all around it delicate forget-me-nots, phecelia, avens, and a host of others lifted their brilliant blooms to the sun.

In June and July the timberline basins are truly a paradise of alpine and sub-alpine flowering plants. They blend here and last summer did so in a unique fashion, for the winter snow had been exceptionally heavy and great banks of it still lay in the hollows by mid-summer. Close to the snow the very earliest spring beauty and glacier lillies were blooming, while a few steps away alpine asters, normally a much later flower, were in full bloom. The lingering snow had simulated a mixing of the seasons so that spring and summer plants were blooming together in an unusual and luxurious display.

Nor were the plants the only things affected by this condition, for on a climb up one steep valley towards a high pass, we found ourselves on continuous snow that choked the bottom of the narrow canyon to a depth of fifteen to twenty feet. It was steep, unbroken and delightfully cool on a hot day. The temperatures were characteristic of May but we looked down into July within little more than a mile. What made it even more interesting was a migration of dragonflies flying up towards the summit of the pass – tens of thousands of them motivated by some unexplained urge to travel. But they were obviously very sensitive to the cold lifting off the surface of the snow; a great many were coming down to land, their exquisitely complex flying apparatus apparently freezing up in the high, rare air. I carried one up the side of the canyon and put it on a rock to lie in the warm sun. In a few moments it revived and took off once more to join the stream heading west against a light breeze. Such observations are reminders of how little we really know about the motivations of nature's host of creatures.

At the summit we climbed on bare talus – the whole surface of the ground made up of fine shards of rock broken into a myriad of shapes. Growing there was a rare and beautiful plant, the alpine columbine, its delicately shaped mauve blooms open in clusters atop a short stem. The blooms are roughly the same size as those of its yellow and cream long-stemmed relative so common in the southern Canadian Rockies. But the alpine variety is found in very few places, its most notable location being on the east slope of the divide in the vicinity of Waterton Lakes Park.

This particular region is also the northern limit of bear grass – not really a grass at all, but a lily. In many spots it is the predominant plant, covering the slopes below and at timberline in an almost solid mat. It looks like grass except for its three-foot-tall flowering stem. The only part that is edible to grazers and browsers is the bloom and seed pods, so it is perhaps fortunate that its range is limited both in elevation and latitude. Its leaves are evergreen and it is unmistakable when in bloom, for the flowers are pale cream in a compound head six to eight inches long and they give the appearance of glowing tapers. I have never seen a specimen growing north of Crowsnest Pass.

The timberline zone of the Rockies is the summering range of most species of grazing animals, particularly the males. It is not uncommon to see herds of mule deer bucks in the high basins where they grow their new antlers. While in the velvet, antlers of all the deer species are tender and easily injured so they prefer to stay in country above the thick timber, up in the wind where the flies and mosquitoes are scarce. While the mule deer does prefer the heavy cover of low ground which offers protection for their fawns, the bucks range up in the high, hanging parks with elk, bighorn sheep and occasional goats and moose.

Bert Riggall and I once counted forty-five buck mule deer in one basin at the head of a burned-out creek, a tributary of the Oldman River at the foot of the divide. Another time I sat on a mountain top on the crest of the McDonald Range, the divide between the Flathead and Wigwam rivers, and without moving counted seventy-five mule deer bucks here and there on both sides of the mountain. Some of them wore enormous racks still in velvet in early September.

Like the mule deer does, cow elk drop their calves in the dense thickets of the lower valleys. A gregarious animal, this is the only time they leave the security of the herd, each cow seeking out her own birthing place. For like the deer, the calves go through a period when they are wobbly and slow on their feet. But just as soon as the calves can keep up, they head for timberline country where they can be observed loafing, feeding and playing all summer long in the flower-strewn meadows. It is not uncommon to see elk, mule deer and sheep mingling in one basin with perhaps a few goats ranging at the foot of the cliffs at the last fringe of trees and a moose or two in the alder thickets on the low side.

From northern British Columbia and Alberta to the Arctic coast, the elk and mule deer give way to the caribou. While the limit of goat range is about two hundred miles north of the sixtieth parallel, the moose thrive as far north as timber grows and even beyond. North of the Peace River, the bighorns are replaced by the handsome dark-coated stone sheep, which in turn fade out to the snow-white dalls in the Mackenzie and Macmillan ranges.

On more occasions than I can remember I have camped among meadows high in the mountains all the way from the international boundary to the northern Yukon Territories. Each location has something unique – some aspect of its geological make-up that makes it memorable. Or one encounters some fairyland combination: bubbling springs flowing down like fountains among exquisite alpine flower gardens designed and tended by the loving hand of nature, where animals and birds play and feed.

There is wood to burn, shelter for the tent, plenty of berries to pick in season and sometimes trout to be taken from a mountain lake. One can stand and watch the ever changing light subtly rearrange the features of great peaks, the draperies of mist parting to reveal scenes of indescribable beauty. If it could be my privilege to pick a heaven where the spirits of mountain men could roam and wander, free and happy forever, it would be the timberline country of the Canadian Rockies in summer and fall.

76 Black bears are not always black, but come in colours ranging from cream through brown to obsidian. A jet black mother can have cubs of any of these hues, including the cinnamon shade of this youngster.

77 Bighorn rams proudly display their great curled weapons. These were photographed at Morro Peak, Jasper National Park.

78 A solitary tree, its foothold precariously shallow, breaks the starkness of glacier-scoured rock.

79 The first touches of autumn's frost paints the aspens along the lower valleys in bright gold.

80 A hard rock formation, standing firm against an old mountain glacier which flattened the terrain to both sides, is today known as the Nunnatok, and is located in the extreme southeast corner of British Columbia.

81 Mount Niles in Yoho Park slumbers under a brilliant moon.

82 Some unknown poet once said, "On yon great cloud and mountain wall are God's great pictures hung." The quotation often comes to mind at sunset in the Rockies when the scene defies description.

83 Here the setting sun fires the summit of Mount Lefroy on the continental divide between Banff and Yoho national parks. The mountain was named for P. S. Lefroy who was killed on this peak in 1896.

84 Mount Fisher, decorated by snow and frost, overlooks historic Fort Steele in British Columbia. David Thompson was likely the first white man to see it towering at the head of Wildhorse Creek.

85 Like an ornament of glittering ice, Angel Glacier sprawls on the north slope of Mount Edith Cavell south of Jasper townsite.

86 A young mule deer buck poses for the photographer in Waterton Lakes National Park.

87 This scree slope below a mountain face attests to the continual erosion of solid rock by snow, rain, wind and changing temperatures.

88 The pika is a small animal that makes its home in rock slides and is often seen and heard by the mountain traveller. It resembles the South American chinchilla but is not related.

89 The high alplands of Jonas Pass in Jasper National Park is one vast carpet of brilliant mountain flowers broken here and there by crystal clear streams and lakes.

90 The wild geranium is a common flower found in the lower foothills and valley floors. Its blooms are generally pink and rarely, white.

91 Alberta's floral emblem, the western wild rose grows all through the Rockies, often in great profusion and to a height of five feet in some regions.

92 The yellow columbine displays its graceful blooms from meadows below timberline to those far above.

93 With its throat shaped like a delicately decorated slipper, the tiny calypso orchid blooms in deep shade under the evergreens at valley level.

94 The western anemone holds aloft its back-lit tufts of seeds that are equally decorative as its blooms.

95 Brilliant Indian paintbrush and yarrow mix their blooms in a mountain meadow.

96 The sticky wet snow of an early fall storm may melt in the warmth of Indian summer but while it lasts it forms a graceful pattern along a mountain stream.

97 The surface of a slow-moving glacier opens in a gaping crevasse. Crevasses may be hidden under the snow surface and can be a death trap for the unwary climber.

98 The Illecillewaet névé – a névé being the snow that lies on the upper reaches of a glacier in the process of turning into ice by the pressure of its own weight.

99 A detailed pattern of fresh snow on the west-facing slabs of Mount Cory in the Sawback Range of Banff National Park.

100 Climbers slogging their way up the last reaches to the summit of Lynx Mountain, located just south of Mount Robson.

101 From the top of the south ridge of Mount Colin the photographer looks out across a vast ocean of undulating mist with islands of peaks revealed here and there.

102 Boom Lake in Banff National Park just north of Vermilion Pass.

103 Numbers One, Three and Four of the Ten Peaks, from the edge of a small lake near the top of Sentinel Pass in Jasper National Park.

104 A typical hanging glacier on Mount Resplendent not far from Mount Robson. Ice falls – dangerous to climbers – occur sporadically on such faces and their thunder can sometimes be heard for miles.

105 A wide and delightfully varied vista overlooking Egypt, Scarab and Mummy lakes from the summit of South Pharoah Peak west of Banff.

106 Various species of lichens often flourish on the surface of rocks even at high altitudes. They assist in the slow process of converting coarse rock to finer sand and gravel.

107 The play of light and shadow on the sawtooth ridge of rocks under the summit of Warrior Mountain form dramatic contrasts.

108 Smoke from a distant forest fire reflects the setting sun over Mount Wilcox near the south boundary of Jasper National Park.

109 At the end of a long day a vivid sunset invites one to sit and watch the rapidly changing colours over the border country of Waterton-Glacier International Peace Park.

110 A bull moose in the rut can be a belligerent animal. This one charged just as the shutter clicked, but the photographer won the footrace to the nearest tree.

111 A downy young eaglet on a bed of fir twigs in a nest hung on a crag between sky and earth is not an easy photographic subject. Beside the bird is an unhatched egg, likely infertile.

112 The view of the valley looking down towards the Whirlpool in Jasper National Park.

113 Storm clouds blow over the mountains behind the lower Bow Valley. In winter such weather usually signals a chinook – a warm wind that can lift temperatures dramatically in a matter of a few hours.

114 Turbulent September storm clouds over Redoubt Lake carry light snow that speckles the country, typical of the restless weather at this time of year.

115 Looking across an alpine pond at the towering wall of the Ramparts. It is summer, when the mountain meadows are spangled with brilliantly coloured wildflowers.

76

78

80

79

81

82

83

84

85

86

90

91

92

93

94

97

98

101

102

103

104

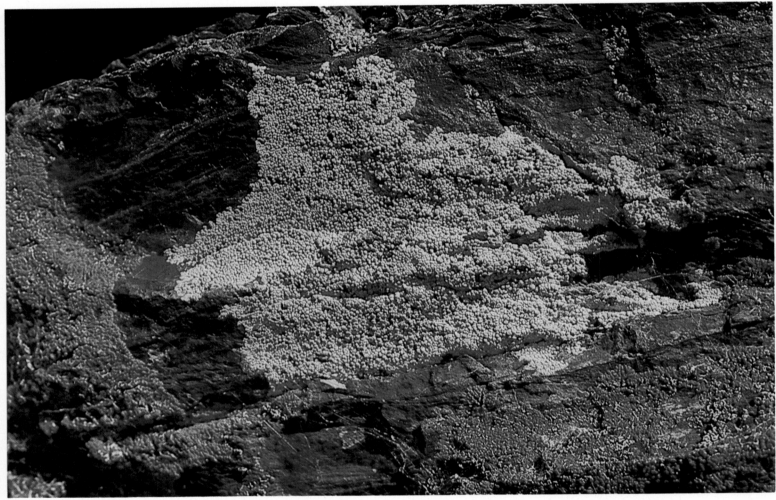

107

108

109

111

112

113

114

The many features of a mountain, from the timber-clad depths of its valleys to the cloud-draped crest of its topmost spire, speak of power, an abiding spirit, and majesty. It is cloaked with the mystique of its past and alive with the life that abounds on it. Ignorance of this is unfortunate, for if we are interested enough to stand at the feet of the gods, we should also be sufficiently concerned to recognize the significance of what it is we see.

The great boulder field, sprawled in a mass of confusion from the base of the cliffs down past timberline, will cease to be just a bone-breaking hazard and unwelcome barrier across the trail. For this is concrete evidence of a mountain in the making. Sometime in the past there were massive forces at work here. The mountain was heaved up from the crust of the earth, forming a fault fronted by a huge turret or wall that teetered on the brink of breaking off. Perhaps an earth tremor or natural erosion tripped its precarious footing and it fell with an earth-shaking roar, filling the air with dust and the acrid smell of brimstone, and carving a new and permanent feature on the face of the parent mountain.

Rockslides of major proportions are comparatively rare, although they will continue to occur here and there as long as the Rockies stand. In my years of wilderness wandering in the high country there have been only two large enough to change the contours of familiar peaks to a noticeable extent. In August 1928, one of the turrets of Castle Mountain, near the head of the river bearing the same name, broke loose to fall onto a lower flank with a thundering boom that was heard for miles. In August 1973, a corner of the face of Chief Mountain, visible from my window as I write this, cracked free to drop and come to rest in a pile of rubble at its foot.

The greatest rockslide of the Rockies recorded in recent history occurred in 1903 in Crowsnest Pass, when two-thirds of the entire front of Turtle Mountain broke loose early one morning, burying the small mining town of Frank and damming the Crowsnest River. The cascading stream of rock finally came to rest with its tip reaching out a mile and a half from the mountain. One of the few survivors of the disaster was an infant girl. She was thrown out of a house that was reduced to kindling within seconds and was later found by a search party, still in her crib and unhurt. Seventy years later I met her quite by chance on a ferry plying the channels between Vancouver and Victoria.

With typical optimism, Frank was rebuilt below the remaining section of the north face of Turtle Mountain. Its residents live there apparently unperturbed by the knowledge that a large crack up on the summit threatens to dump the rest of the peak on them. A sizable hotel was built and in its gift shop tourists buy booklets and postcards featuring the historic event.

Such a confusion of smashed rock looks lifeless, but this is an illusion, for plants will grow anywhere that the soil allows roots to take hold. The irregularity of the rock offers a multitude of hides for small animals, which in turn attract birds and other animals that prey on them.

A friend and I once sat in a patch of shintangle fir watching pikas, ground squirrels and marmots feeding, playing and otherwise going about their business on the edge of a rockslide. All but the ground squirrels made their dens among the loose boulders and fed at the edges of adjoining meadows. The tumbled boulders gave them cover and a sense of security, even if they were not completely safe from predators.

We had our glasses trained on a small patch of grass about a hundred yards away along the edge of the slide, where three half-grown marmots were frolicking. Overlooking their play and keeping an eye out for danger was one of the parents on sentry duty. When we had taken up our observation post we had disturbed them and they greeted us with the long-drawn, piercing whistle of alarm so familiar in mountain country. We were still closely watched by the keen eyes of the old marmot on the rock, but had apparently been appraised as more or less harmless, for within a few minutes of our arrival the young marmots had come out to play.

Now they were rolling about in a carefree fashion, occasionally stopping to nibble at grass. At one point we saw two of them rear up, chest to chest with forepaws clasping each other and cheeks pressed together, and rock back and forth in what appeared to be a demonstration of fraternal affection. It was a serene and happy scene typical of the high country on a pleasant summer afternoon.

Without warning a big golden eagle shot into view and made a low level pass that just cleared a bulge in the boulder field behind the big marmot. In the twinkling of an eye the bird dove to strike, but its shadow gave it away an instant too soon. The wicked, curved claws just missed their mark as the marmot tumbled off the rock to the side with a gurgling whistle of panic. The big bird checked in a towering turn and spotted the young marmots falling all over themselves in a wild scramble for their den. The moment of mutual surprise saved them, for before the eagle could change direction for another strike, they were swallowed by the earth under a rock. The eagle swooped away in search of other prey to feed its hungry young in a nest somewhere on the face of the peak behind us.

We swung our glasses slowly back and forth across the sprawling basin. High on the ridge rimming its far side we spotted a bunch of bighorn ewes and their lambs bedded in a strip of loose talus. Behind them higher still against the sky there appeared three big rams. For a while they stood motionless side by side, their great curling horns silhouetted against the blue, then they too bedded down, the picture of relaxed indolence. Like the eagle and the marmots, they are endowed with extraordinary vision and there is not much by way of life on the slopes that escapes their notice.

For a while we amused ourselves watching the ever busy pikas gathering hay that grew in scattered clumps through the rock slide for their stacks of winter forage. Aside from those standing watch on the tops of outlook rocks, they were forever on the move. Tiny animals that will fit in the palm of a hand, their fine furred coats blend so completely with the rock that they seem to disappear like magic before one's eyes.

Not large enough to be of interest to eagles, the pikas are nonetheless wary, for they are preyed upon by the smaller hawks. But their arch-enemies are the weasel and the occasional martin, for these sinuous, lightning fast hunters can pursue them to the innermost crannies of their hides among the rocks. More than once I have watched a weasel searching through a rock slide for pikas and his intrusion will be well known to the animals in the vicinity in an instant. Every pika will be up on top of the nearest prominence sounding off a steady alarm of squeaky bleats.

Ground squirrels will react in the same way. I have seen one perched atop a stump left by an avalanche that had broken off the upper trunk. There it sat on a spot no more than three inches wide and five feet from the ground, giving off a stream of shrill barks. One feels the sheer terror in their alarm and the tension in the air when the deadly weasel is present. No doubt any young still underground suffer heavy casualties, for the weasel is a compulsive killer and will prey on its victims long after its belly is full.

My friend and I sat back in lazy comfort against a springy cushion of boughs, basking in the sun and enjoying the scene before us. Occasionally we spoke in low tones, but most of the time we just watched while cloud shadows slipped across the slopes near and far.

Out of the corner of my eye I saw something move down at the foot of the slide in some scrubby timber by a shallow creek. We trained our glasses on the spot, but could see nothing at first. I had decided it must have been my imagination when a fine silvertip grizzly ambled out into the lush meadow. Then a pair of cubs – probably two-year-olds – trailed her into view as they fed. One wore a magnificent honey-blonde coat with dark ears, face and underparts, while the other was a nondescript brown. The bears were announced by the long whistle of a marmot across the basin and another from the top of a boulder near us.

The big bears occasionally turn to marmot hunting when the rodent has gone into hibernation in the fall. The bears excavate huge holes to get down to the nesting chamber and their success depends on the marmots' choice of location. If the digging is easy, the bear dines on rich, fat meat, but when subterranean boulders block the way there is nothing but frustration. Even though such deaths most often occur when the marmots are in the deep coma of hibernation, they associate grizzlies with danger and I have often located a bear by taking note of a marmot's whistle of alarm.

If the bears before us were aware of the disturbance they were causing, they showed no sign of it. They are the true monarchs of the mountains among the four-footed creatures.

Before the white man arrived with his long rifle, the grizzly was supreme; very rarely did the Indians challenge these surprisingly quick, powerful animals. Some of the tribes believed that there was a kinship between man and bear, a belief which is not unjustified for a skinned bear looks disturbingly like a man. When the occasional grizzly bear was killed, it was the custom of many tribes that the hunter prayed to the spirit of the bear begging forgiveness. Among the Old Crow Indians of the Porcupine River flats, along the western rim of the northern Rockies, it is still a tradition among elder hunters that a man must possess very special medicine to kill a bear. Within the memory of the oldest ones there were such hunters, men who pursued the grizzlies into their dens and killed them with a knife. They claim that a grizzly will not fight in its den – a theory that will likely remain unchallenged, for even the most zealous researcher has his limitations.

One cannot watch grizzlies feeding and rambling through their mountain habitat without a feeling of awe. They are the living epitome of power, an animal whose sagacity and courage are pre-eminent among all others in the wilderness. To watch one take a great clawed paw and heave a good-sized rock out of the ground with ease is to be impressed. And the more one observes the bears, the more one is convinced of their intelligence.

While all mountain travellers are aware of the presence of grizzlies in the Canadian Rockies, there is no reason to be inordinately afraid. Some common-sense precautions will usually prevent an uncomfortable confrontation. In spite of the numbers of people using the parks for recreation, few grizzlies are encountered. The possibility of being injured by a bear is far more remote than the chance of traffic injury. One rule that we have always observed over many years of living in and travelling through grizzly country is never run from a bear; to do so only invites pursuit that may end in tragedy. Besides which, nobody can run fast enough to outdistance a bear. The best way to handle a close-range confrontation is to back off diplomatically, always facing the bear, with no sudden motions of panic. It takes some self-control, but it is by far the safest course. In all likelihood the surprise has been mutual and a grizzly generally welcomes the chance to save face and avoid trouble when offered an alternative.

The grizzlies in front of us were moving our way, the mother in the lead and the cubs lined up at her heels. They came directly up the slope, crossing the meadow flanking the rock slide until they reached a strip of huckleberry brush. This came in for some examination, but the berries were still too small and green to be of much interest. The big mother made a cursory examination of a ground squirrel hole, dug a couple of sods out of its doorway and sniffed it, but apparently decided that any further digging would be a waste of effort.

There was a big boulder about six feet high and twice as wide lying by itself to one side of the slide and when they came to it the she-bear ambled around behind it and proceeded to climb up on top. For several minutes she stood broadside to us in sharp profile against the mountains beyond, a classic picture of regal dignity.

Meanwhile the cubs were gambolling down slope to one side of her, and a vagrant puff of air must have given them our scent. Their instant reaction was one of keen attention rather than fear, a transformation from the completely relaxed to the wary. They looked to their mother, but she was paying no attention, so they moved close to her rock and one climbed up beside her. She turned, recognizing the change of mood, and touched noses with the cub very briefly. Beyond that fleeting contact we can only guess at the kind of communication exchanged. But the message was unmistakable, for the next moment the big bear bounded off the rock, leading the way at a long gallop back toward the thick timber along the creek.

It had been a fascinating afternoon for us, a few memorable hours that one enjoys now and then on the rugged face of a mountain. On such occasions when it is my privilege to observe this procession of life, sometimes recording part of the action on film, it is always a satisfaction to be part of the scene rather than in conflict with it.

Such days demonstrate that mountains are anything but inanimate lumps standing up against the sky, but rather nature's monuments to the life they support. And if we hope to keep them thus, we must recognize that this life is fragile, requiring our constant vigilance to prevent damage that cannot be erased.

Among Cliffs and Pinnacles

It was morning. One of the hunting eagles came sloping in at a long angle, cutting through the thermal that was lifting along the face of a mountain wall. The bird flew like a flung javelin, at sizzling speed, wings set in a quarter fold, and it headed for the nest where two well-grown fledglings waited for their first feed of the day. Its angle of descent took it a bit below the nest of coarse sticks built on a small, jutting pinnacle. A few yards out it set its wings to check its speed and swooped up to toss a ground squirrel into the nest with perfectly timed precision. Then the bird towered and folded its wings for a split second stop, banked over sharply to plummet down along the face of the cliff, and swooped back across the thermal. Planing off, the bird's keen eyes spotted its mate coming in with another ground squirrel caught in its talons.

It was the beginning of the daily feeding routine, a shuttling back and forth between the nest and a grassy ridge a mile or so down the valley where ground squirrels abounded. The hunting was periodically interrupted with spells of flying for the sheer love of playing in the wind, when the eagle spiralled up in a rapidly lifting thermal until it became a mere speck in the blue sky. It was joined there by its mate and the pair of them swung in great circles, free and unfettered as the mountain air that is their element, while back at the nest their hungry young tore chunks from the squirrels, gulped them down and chirped for more.

These are the masters of the mountain heights: fierce, bold, completely predacious. In the feathered world the golden eagle along with its relative, the bald eagle, share the apex.

Their life span is a long one, reaching as many as seventy years, but the nature of their ways precludes large populations, for they are slow breeders even under the most ideal conditions. Their only real enemy is man, who once killed them for head-dress feathers and now destroys them in fancied protection of domestic sheep wintering across the southern plains and deserts. Others die in a puff of smoke when trying to perch on high tension power lines, and some are poisoned by baits set out for coyotes. They are at home and unmolested in summer while nesting in the high crags and cliffs of the Rockies.

These crags and cliffs are also the summer homesteads of other winged specialists, and amongst these is the rare and beautiful black swift.

They are the little masters of the air, exquisitely agile and graceful in flight. In forty years of travelling through the high mountains along the main spine of the Rockies I have seen them only twice in the extreme southeastern corner of British Columbia.

I once camped for the night under some tall spruce and woke before the sun touched the face of the peak towering up on the far side of Ashman Lake. I was snug and comfortable in my sleeping robe and lay there looking up through a space in the tops of the spruces at a pale blue patch of sky. Then came a hint of movement away up at the extreme limits of my vision. I reached for the binoculars hung on a knot above the head of my bed and focused them on a flock of birds wheeling and circling far overhead. Their outline and colouration were unmistakably those of the black swift, a bird that makes its nest high on the inaccessible faces of towering cliffs. As far as I know, nobody has yet photographed a nest of this bird with eggs or young in it. Indeed, very few observers have had a good close-up view of the bird.

Another small bird one meets in the high country where the snow-drifts linger till late summer is the grey-capped rosy finch. Many times over the years I have seen this cheerful little one busily searching along the edge of a snowdrift, picking up insects that have stalled out in the chill or seeds that have blown in with the snow during winter hurricanes. Once when I was sitting comfortably in a patch of heather eating my lunch, one of these trusting birds flew off a nearby snowdrift and landed on the upturned toe of my boot. Its feet must have been cold for it ruffled its feathers and settled down to warm its toes against its breast, meanwhile watching me with bright eyes as I slowly munched a sandwich.

This bird also hides its nest in nooks and crannies among chimneys and breaks on the cliffs. And it too will provide a possible first for the intrepid photographer with a head for heights and a sharp eye for detail. A picture of a rosy finch on its nest would be a jewel in anyone's collection of nature photographs.

In summer the high country is subject to a variety of weather ranging from that expected of paradise to wind and storms as violent as any found on earth. Yet the birds that nest there happily endure these periods of harshness. The one bird that lives here all the year round and can be found from high alplands to timberline is the ptarmigan. In the southern Canadian

Rockies one will see the white-tailed variety; farther north, the rock or arctic ptarmigan predominates. These birds nest in the short alpine tundra, where their summer plumage camouflages them so effectively that they are very difficult to spot, even when almost under foot. They raise their broods there with wary eyes on the watch for eagles. Let one of the big birds wheel into view and the mother will give a low chirping call that freezes every bird in the covey. At such times they are reluctant to fly – so much so that it is possible to pick them up. More than once I have confounded guests by waiting till an eagle showed up, then walking in amongst ptarmigan and catching one in my hands with no great difficulty.

When winter snows begin to blanket the land in late fall, the ptarmigan changes its dress to pure white. While waiting out a heavy snow squall in the lee of a cornice near the top of Plateau Mountain, a friend and I watched a whole covey of ptarmigan parade out of the storm into the shelter of a hollow in front of us. Except for a few dark feathers scattered on the breasts of two or three, all were in snowy winter garb rendering them almost invisible but for their black eyes and beaks. Those wearing the dark coloured feathers seemed to be aware of their imperfect camouflage, for we saw one bird pluck several of them out and discard them in the snow.

The standing-on-end country of the high Rockies is spectacular in its geography, rich in its history and fascinating in the wildlife it contains. Unlike the high country of Nepal, Tibet and South America, where people and animals live up to and above ten thousand feet, the Rockies have few permanent human residents above five thousand feet, and the variety of larger animals is relatively limited. The climate at this altitude is sub-arctic and winter snows are deep; in some regions winter winds reach hurricane velocities. It can be an extremely harsh and inhospitable environment, lashed by wild storms and cannonaded by avalanches.

The mountain goat winters successfully on some of the high, wind-whipped ridges under conditions that would kill less hardy species. At times these animals descend to lower levels and graze off the tree lichens put within reach by deep, crusted snow that will support their weight.

The cliffs are escape terrain for the goats, a part of their habitat that protects them from all predators, with the exception of the eagle, occasional wolverine, and man with his long-range rifle. No wolf or coyote will tackle a goat – even an immature one – on the steep rock. The cougar, a most adept and surefooted climber in its own right, will not stalk a goat in such country, but will wait till it moves to more favourable ground. Apart from its marvelous skill as a climber, the goat is a coolheaded and formidable fighter with stiletto sharp horns, and has been known to kill a grizzly in combat though it lost its own life in the battle.

The golden eagle will sometimes take a small kid, but the young stay close to their mothers most of the time and at the first threat of attack promptly take shelter under her belly. Sometimes individual eagles will learn to strike mature goats when they are crossing a very narrow ledge on the face of a cliff. The sudden jolt of the big bird hitting them on the back tips them off into space and they are dashed to their deaths on the rocks below, where the eagle proceeds to feed on the ragged remains. Twice I have seen eagles make a determined try for mature goats in this manner, but both times the animal escaped by quickly leaping to a spot where there was room to fight off the attack.

The less precipitous parts of this escape terrain are shared with the wild sheep in summer, who find it not only a discouragement to predators, but also a shelter from the heat of the sun. Indeed, the big rams often live in the high green hanging basins, growing fat on an exotic diet of alpine flora and it is not uncommon to see them feeding belly deep in brilliant blooms.

I have seen them playing follow the leader exactly as humans play the game, only they choose to defy gravity with a kind of fast footwork so dazzling it is hard to follow in the dust that is raised. Or they sometimes choose to play it on a steep-pitched snowdrift, climbing up and glissading down in a continuous round. The long drop of a perpendicular cliff at the lower edge of the drift worries them not at all.

The mighty grizzly also winters in the high country but snoozes away the cold months in a snug den sometimes as much as forty feet under the surface of the snow. The cubs are born in the den in mid-January, tiny mites weighing only about sixteen ounces, practically hairless, blind and helpless. There they stay till May or early June, sucking rich milk and growing prodigiously. When they emerge into the spring sunshine they weigh twenty to twenty-four pounds each and are fully furred, miniature grizzlies with all their senses tuned.

Most of the rodents that live on the high slopes – ground squirrels, chipmunks and marmots – are true hibernators, spending six to nine months in a deep coma with their breathing barely perceptible and heart action reduced to four or five beats per minute. The tiny chipmunk, smallest of all the squirrels, hibernates as high as ten thousand feet above sea level in some crack or niche in solid rock. The energetic pikas stay awake all winter, travelling back and forth between their small haystacks amongst the loose rock under the snow, and not surfacing until spring. Whatever their winter habits, summer is a period of great activity for all.

There is little feed to attract a grizzly for very long above timberline in summer, but they are excellent climbers and can be seen on occasion traversing very steep faces between buttress ridges. One fall three companions and I were glassing the front of a steep mountain overlooking a small alpine lake, when we spotted what looked like a bear sleeping in the deep shade up near the summit.

It was far enough away that we could not make a positive identification, even through powerful binoculars. I suggested that we watch it a while and if it did not move it was likely just a trick of shadow on the rock ledge, for the general rule says to watch something you suspect is a bear for ten minutes and if it remains motionless, it is something else.

But such rules have their exceptions. Thirty minutes later the shadow resolved itself into a big grizzly that got up, shook itself and headed out along the ledge to disappear around the corner of the mountain. No doubt the animal had been feeding on some choice huckleberry patch above timberline and had climbed up to that cool, shady place to sleep away the hot hours of the afternoon.

Grizzly bears can be found almost anywhere in the mountains and there are several recorded sightings on the larger icefields. I once followed a mother grizzly with a yearling cub for miles across the great snowfield at the head of the Illecillewaet River in the Selkirk Mountains of British Columbia. She had some definite though faraway objective in mind for she never rested or deviated from her chosen course.

Mountain wildlife reaches into every fold of the towering, austere peaks – even out onto the cold expanses of ice and snow. The wonderful endurance of these creatures is the promise of nature's continuing bounty.

The Tapestry of Nature

When we walk through the Rockies' wilderness areas we are surrounded by nature's artistry. Here are formations and patterns that have evolved over millions of years, compositions and colours so daring, brilliant and overwhelming they literally leave us breathless. Be it sculpted stone or a fawn's markings it commands our awe and, more important, our respect.

Perhaps the most satisfying and thrilling experiences I have ever known in a long career associated very closely with wilderness country have been those occasions when I have been accepted by wild things as a friendly part of their environment. For then they are unafraid and together we have enjoyed the use of the surroundings with no stress or strife. Even the mighty grizzly will tolerate a man at close range, without any show of belligerence or concern, when the man comes with an open heart, without weapons.

I recall some wonderful days when I was allowed to travel with a female grizzly and her cubs in an atmosphere of mutual trust. No wild thing – especially a big mother bear, powerful and arrogant in her own right and justifiably solicitous and protective of her cubs – can pay a man any greater compliment. For he is a well-established enemy, the only one she can really count, and furthermore he smells very bad to her sensitive nose under the best of circumstances.

Nobody in his right mind would attempt such liberties without first introducing himself and finding out if the bear will show any tolerance. These overtures call for much patience for no two grizzlies are alike. They are just as individualistic as people and possess their own marked preferences. The preliminaries in this case took some time, and my sons and I camped in her vicinity for several days. At first we made our presence known at some distance, gradually closing the range and watching her reaction. How many times she investigated us with her wonderful nose we will never know. But when she finally chose to accept us and ignore our presence, it was to us a thrill and a privilege.

Walk with me through a mountain valley among tall trees, along a brawling, tumbling stream and see a dipper curtsying on a rock awash in the current before stepping into the crystal clear water to hunt bugs among the pebbles on the bottom. Collecting a beakful, she flies to her nest, cunningly constructed of moss, on a tiny ledge under an overhang close by a falls where fine spray plays over it almost continually. She too is a specialist – one that makes use of the water for protection and as a source of food.

Up above the falls among some broken outcrops in the same rock face, a brilliant blue male mountain bluebird follows his mate with a collection of bugs to feed their young in a nest hidden away in a niche. In the full glare of a shaft of sunlight, he is a brilliant feathered jewel in comparison to the softer pastel colours of the female.

Our trail takes us on up to timberline, to the rock slides and talus fans and to the high cliffs of the peak beyond, and if we have learned to move in pace with our surroundings we see and learn many things. It is a revelation to find that this is the key to acceptance, that we are not always treated with fear and timidity by other kinds of life we may meet. Above all we become aware that the mountains are themselves a paradox. From a distance the peaks appear to be relatively untouched by the encroachments of man; they are still big, wild and indescribably primitive and their general features and outline seem untouched. Indeed man's settlements and his exploits appear to be mere scratches on their faces here and there across a vastness that has endured for ages.

But when our souls have become steeped in their magic and our eyes and minds have become attuned to their rhythm, we can see all too clearly that man-made pressures have had a profound effect on the lives of the wild things found here. It is a disturbing discovery, and perhaps we walk more softly in sympathy, wondering if such animals as the grizzly, completely dependent on true wilderness habitat, will ultimately disappear. Those of us who have known the Rockies for three or four decades have seen the goat leave much of its former range. We have seen the magnificent elk wane to a point of scarcity in valleys that should encourage its proliferation. And we wonder sometimes about our own future here.

We who have lived in the Rockies long enough to make comparisons have observed shocking changes in a few short years. Man's incomprehensible destruction during the past fifty years alone emerges as the most devastating force to fall on the land since the ice ages. The era of human supremacy is but a fraction of those centuries since life first began, yet the tracks we have left are dangerously deep and almost totally indelible.

We know that the upper reaches of our watersheds are vital to human survival, yet we overgraze the grass cover, clean out the timber right down to the stream banks, and then compound the folly by building dams to catch the resulting silt. We know that minerals and petroleum are non-renewable – once they are gone they are vanished forever – yet we call for more and more and too often tear these resources from the earth in a careless fashion, without counting the costs of the long range impact on every kind of life. It is worse that just destructive; it is self-destructive. It is a game where the quick and ruthless are ultimately paid in hard coin and the devil takes the hindmost – and the hindmost eventually includes everyone. If the outcome were not so grim and irreversible, it would be laughable.

We romanticize the freedom and open space of the wilderness and extol its aesthetic and recreational value; we cry for clean water and pure air. Yet we destroy the life systems that make possible these blessings. So far we have not understood that it is our own demand for more energy, more building materials, more soft-living amenities, that thwarts such aspirations. When will we wake up to the sure knowledge that we cannot take forever, without plan and consideration for the future? Will those who profess to know and love the Rockies make their voices heard?

When the last grizzly and mountain goat are gone and the wilderness lies gutted and open to the sun, man will be looking at his own sad conclusion – the price of his own selfish disregard.

The old and poignant photographer's prayer comes to mind, "Please, God, let there be light!"

Notes on the Photographers

Robert Ashburner, a native of Calgary, Alberta, is a park naturalist in Banff National Park. He graduated from the University of Calgary with a B.Sc. in zoology in 1972 and since that time has been employed by Parks Canada. He skies and hikes extensively in the mountain national parks. **Plates 4, 8, 45.**

Donald Beers, hiker, climber and naturalist, teaches school in Calgary, Alberta. He was introduced to photography and to the mountains by his friend Leonard Leacock. Mr. Beers's photographs have appeared in publications in North America and in Europe. **Plates 5, 9, 10, 13, 14, 17, 59, 60, 97, 100, 102, 103, 104, 105, 108, 115.**

Egon Bork is a graduate student at the University of Alberta. His work has appeared in publications for the Canadian Government Travel Bureau, in the *Canadian Geographical Journal, North, The Beaver* and in the centennial volume *Canada: A Year of the Land,* produced by the National Film Board of Canada. Mr. Bork is a native of Germany. **Plates 6, 43, 79.**

Edward J. R. Cavell is compiling an overview of photography in western Canada from 1850 to 1880 with the assistance of the Canada Council. Born in 1948 in Lachine, Quebec, he attended Mt. Allison University in New Brunswick for a short time before moving to Banff in 1968 where he held various jobs, from fire lookout to cook. He graduated in 1973 from the visual communications program at the Banff Centre School of Fine Arts and has since been working in Banff. **Plates 3, 31.**

John S. Crawford is a full time free-lance wildlife cameraman and outdoor writer currently working on a wolf study in the Canadian Rockies. Born in Seattle, he graduated from the University of Michigan. His photographs have appeared in publications of the National Museum of Canada, the Department of Indian Affairs and Northern Development, the United States Department of the Interior, and in numerous nature books and outdoor magazines. **Plates 16, 24, 25.**

German-born Helga Dauer is a free-lance photographer living in Calgary, Alberta. A hiker and skier, she is an outdoor enthusiast; when she became interested in photography six years ago and completed the Famous Pho-

tographers School course, her interests merged. She has won awards in national and international photography competitions for her work. **Plates 65, 82, 90, 92, 95.**

A photographer, former climbing guide and ski instructor, Bruno Engler has spent most of his life in the Canadian Rockies since he emigrated from his native Switzerland in 1939. He learned mountaineering in the Alps and photography from his father, also a photographer, and later studied at a Swiss art school. Still active in both areas—in winter he is a ski patrolman at Lake Louise—he has travelled widely with the American Broadcasting Corporation filming sports events. In 1968 the National Film Board asked him to act as technical advisor for a film which was based on an idea he submitted, *A Mountain is a Living Thing.* **Plates 1, 41, 57, 76.**

Former park warden Hans Fuhrer is now an alpine specialist in the Yukon's Kluane National Park. Photography and mountain climbing are his hobbies; taking his camera along, he makes frequent climbs and hikes into the remoter regions of the park. He immigrated to Canada in 1963 from his native Switzerland. **Plates 89, 110.**

Tom W. Hall has travelled 300,000 miles by jeep through western Canada, taking photographs since his retirement from the electronics business in 1962. He has a collection of over 50,000 prints relating to natural science, and his work has been published internationally. **Plate 21.**

Zoologist Dr. Cy Hampson is one of Canada's foremost wildlife photographers. Working with his wife Mary, he uses black and white film, 35mm colour transparencies and 16mm movie film to record subjects ranging from single-celled organisms to plants and animals. Dr. Hampson's intent is to capture photographically the essence of his subjects and to present them with appreciation and enthusiasm. His work has been published internationally and has won awards for excellence in photography. **Plates 30, 66, 106.**

Mary Hampson, natural history enthusiast and photographer, ranks with her husband Cy Hampson as one of Canada's outstanding wildlife photographers. When not in the field with cameras, much of her time is spent developing and enlarging black and white prints in the darkroom, cataloguing their 35mm slide collection, or editing 16mm movie film. **Page 1; Plates 26, 47, 85.**

George Hunter specializes in industrial and travel photographs and is one of the last large-format photographers in Canada, producing colour transparencies 4" x 5" and 5" x 7" in size. He divides his time between commissioned assignments and travels across Canada securing photos for his stock colour library. The National Film Board selected one hundred of his colour prints of people for the film *People of Many Lands.* **Plates 2, 33, 64.**

Edi Klopfenstein works for the CNR in Jasper National Park and is a free-lance photographer. He was born in Adelboden, Switzerland, in 1945. After a three-year apprenticeship he worked as a photographer prior to his immigration to Canada in 1968. **Plates 11, 20, 28, 42, 54, 63, 101, 112.**

Although J. A. Kraulis is a relative newcomer to photography, he has seen his work published in several periodicals and has fulfilled travel assignments in western Canada, Europe and Lebanon. He has backpacked, ski-toured, climbed and canoed in many American and Canadian wilderness areas, but after seeing the Canadian Rockies for the first time nine years ago considers them his favourite part of the world and returns to them yearly from his home in Montreal where he is pursuing studies in architecture. **Jacket; pages 2/3, 4 lower left, 4 right; plates 7, 15, 29, 32, 34, 35, 36, 37, 39, 44, 46, 48, 49, 50, 52, 53, 55, 58, 62, 71, 73, 74, 78, 81, 83, 87, 93, 94, 96, 113, 114.**

By 1976, Margaret Lewis and her husband Ken, co-founders of Muskeg Productions, will have produced seventeen individual environmental educational films since they began production in Calgary in 1971, three years after immigrating to Canada. A writer as well, she has written articles for several periodicals and has scripted twenty-five plays for radio broadcast. **Plate 69.**

Native Albertan Don McLeod lives in Jasper, Alberta, where he is a locomotive engineer for the CNR. Photography is a hobby to which he devotes considerable time as he hikes and climbs in Jasper National Park. A conservationist, he is interested in and concerned with the preservation of our national parks and wilderness areas. **Page 4 upper left.**

Twenty-three-year-old Patrick Morrow of Kimberley, British Columbia, received a diploma of journalism administration from the Southern Alberta Institute of Technology in Calgary, then served a one-year apprenticeship on the photo staff of the Calgary *Herald.* He later studied visual communications at the Banff Centre School of Fine Arts. **Plates 12, 72, 84, 99.**

A. Charles Russell ranches near Twin Butte, Alberta. He is a graduate of the New York School of Photography and has travelled widely in the wilderness country of western and northern Canada and New Zealand. **Plate 88.**

The Rockies is the fifth book for Andy Russell, internationally renowned naturalist, photographer, lecturer and author. All his books reflect the life-long experience of a man who has been a broncobuster, trapper, professional guide and rancher. Born in 1915 at Lethbridge, Alberta, he grew up on a ranch in the Twin Butte region of the province. **Plates 22, 27, 38, 61, 91, 109.**

H. John Russell is a consultant zoologist. He was born at Pincher Creek, Alberta, in 1944 and later received his formal education at the University of Alberta. He now lives on a small ranch near Waterton Park. **Plate 80.**

Zoologist Richard H. Russell works with the Canadian Wildlife Service in Edmonton, Alberta. Born in 1939 in Pincher Creek, he is a graduate of the University of British Columbia and the University of Alberta. **Plates 51, 67.**

John Steele works as a seasonal park naturalist in Jasper National Park, the most recent of several jobs which have allowed him access to the mountains of western Canada during the past eight years. **Plate 98.**

Free-lance photographer David Trione studied photography at Oregon State University and at the Banff Centre School of Fine Arts. He is an experienced mountaineer, having spent over ten years climbing in the mountains of western North America. A native of Oregon, he was born in 1953 in Eugene and now makes his home in Corvallis. **Plates 40, 56, 75.**

G. W. Vroom researches grizzly bears in Banff National Park as part of a special studies project on wildlife. He joined the warden service in 1955, has lived in and patrolled the remote areas of the park and, being involved in public safety work, has done a great deal of mountain rescue. He was born in 1931 in Pincher Creek to pioneer Alberta ranchers. **Plate 70.**

Thirty-one-year-old Tom Willock, contract biologist in environmental impact studies for the government of Alberta, has worked in the natural history field continuously since 1964. A graduate of the University of Alberta and Carleton University, his publications include twenty research articles in journals and photo stories in *Animals* and *Nature Canada.* **Plates 19, 68, 86, 107, 111.**

Plates 18, 23 and 77 courtesy of Parks Canada.